Johann Georg Kohl, Robert Ralph Noel

A Popular History of the Discovery of America

From Columbus to Franklin. Vol. II

Johann Georg Kohl, Robert Ralph Noel

A Popular History of the Discovery of America
From Columbus to Franklin. Vol. II

ISBN/EAN: 9783744673846

Printed in Europe, USA, Canada, Australia, Japan

Cover: Foto ©ninafisch / pixelio.de

More available books at **www.hansebooks.com**

A POPULAR HISTORY

OF THE

DISCOVERY OF AMERICA,

FROM COLUMBUS TO FRANKLIN.

By J. G. KOHL.

TRANSLATED FROM THE GERMAN

By MAJOR R. R. NOEL.

IN TWO VOLUMES.
VOL. II.

LONDON:
CHAPMAN AND HALL, 193, PICCADILLY.
1862.

CONTENTS OF VOL. II.

CHAPTER I.

THE NAVAL HEROES OF QUEEN ELIZABETH, AND THE EAST COAST OF THE UNITED STATES.

PAGE

John Cabot discovers North America (June 24, anno 1497)—Ponce de Leon discovers Florida (1513)—Coligny's Huguenots in Florida (1562, 1568)—Sir John Hawkins's Expeditions (1562, 1565, 1567)—Sir Francis Drake's Voyage round the World (1577, 1578)—Sir Humphrey Gilbert's first Attempt at Colonisation (1583)— Sir Walter Raleigh's Voyage to Virginia (1584 and 1602)—John Smith Colonises the Bay of Chesapeake (1607)—The Dutch discover New Belgium (New York, 1609)—The Puritans build Boston (1630)—Oxenstierna founds New Sweden on the Delaware (1638)—The English conquer New Belgium (1664)—Penn founds Pennsylvania (1682)—Oglethorpe founds Georgia (1732) 1

CHAPTER II.

THE FRENCH AND THE FUR-HUNTERS IN CANADA.

The Cabots discover the Fish-banks of Newfoundland (anno 1497)—Caspar de Cortereal discovers Labrador (1500)—Giovanni Verazano sails along the Coasts of North America (1524)—Jacques Cartier discovers the Gulf of St. Lawrence (1534)—Jacques Cartier discovers the River St. Lawrence and Canada (1535)—Roberval and Cartier go to Canada (1542)—Roberval and his Fleet disappear (1548)—Samuel Champlain founds Quebec (1608)—Samuel Champlain organises the Province of Canada, and explores the Lower Lakes (1608, 1635)—Father Mesnard discovers the Upper Lakes (1660)—The Jesuits Allouez and Marquette complete the exploration of Lake Superior and Lake Michigan (1666) 58

CHAPTER III.

THE MISSISSIPPI AND THE JESUITS.

The Captains of Governor Garay discover the Mouths of the Mississippi (1519)—Pamphilo de Navaez is lost at the Mouths of the Mississippi (1529)—Cabeza de Vaca wanders about for nine Years in the Lands to the south-west of the Mississippi (1529-1537)—Fernando de Soto discovers and navigates the Lower Mississippi (1540-1542)—Moscoso's Retreat (1543)—The Jesuit Marquette goes down the entire Mississippi in a Canoe (1673) 103

b

CONTENTS.

CHAPTER IV.

THE MARCH OF THE RUSSIANS AND COSSACKS THROUGH SIBERIA TO AMERICA.

PAGE

Annika Stroganoff sends his People over the Ural (anno 1570) — Jermak Timofejeff and his Cossacks ride over the Ural (1578)—Jermak gains Possession of " Sibir" (1580)—The Cossacks reach the Lena (1628)—The Cossacks gain Possession of Kamtschatka (1690-1706)—The Cossacks hear of the " Great Land," (America) (1706)—Peter the Great orders the Discovery of the "Great Land,"(North-West America) (1723)—Behring and Tschirokoff reach America from Siberia (1741)—The Russians take Possession of North-West America (1760) 144

CHAPTER V.

THE NORTH AND THE ENGLISH.

Martin Frobisher's Voyages to "Meta Incognita" (anno 1572-1578)—John Davis discovers Davis's Strait (1585)—Henry Hudson discovers Hudson's Bay (1610)—Bylot and Baffin discover Baffin's Bay (1616)—John Ross begins the Series of Arctic Expeditions of Modern Times (1818)—William Edward Parry penetrates into Lancaster Sound in the American Polar Sea (1816)—Sir John Franklin's Land Journey to the Coasts of the American Polar Sea (1820-21)—Sir John Franklin's last Voyage (1845)—M'Clure discovers the North-West Passage, and proves that America is surrounded by Water (Oct. 1850) 185

CHAPTER VI.

CONCLUDING OBSERVATIONS ON THE RESULTS OF THE DISCOVERY OF AMERICA TO COMMERCE, NAVIGATION, SCIENCE, RELIGION, AND POLITICS.

Introduction of European Diseases—Changes in the Condition and Habits of the Natives of America—Destruction of the American Civilisation—Extinction of the Red Race—Development of New Races — Changes in the Aspect of Nature, and in the Climate through the Cultivation of the Soil and the Introduction of New Animals and Plants: Sugar, Coffee, Cotton, Negro Slavery—Spread of American Plants and Animals in Europe: Potatoes, Tobacco, Maize, Medicines, Turkeys—Changes of Political and Commercial Power and Hegemony in Europe—Zenith of the Power of the Portuguese and Spaniards, and its Decline—Decline of Italian Commerce; of German Commerce; of the Hanse Towns—Freedom of the Netherlands—Rise of the English—Influence on Sciences—Cosmology—Astronomy—Botanical Gardens—Menageries—Natural Sciences—Ethnography—History of Man—Impulse to Invention—Increased Moral and Physical Mobility of European Nations—Modern Languages and Literature—Spread and Stability of the Christian Religion 231

A POPULAR HISTORY

OF THE

DISCOVERY OF AMERICA.

―――♦―――

CHAPTER I.

THE NAVAL HEROES OF QUEEN ELIZABETH, AND THE

ERRATUM.
Vol II., page 161, 4th line from the bottom, *for* "Russia" *read* "China."

Virginia (1584 and 1602)—John Smith Colonises the Bay of Chesapeake (1607)—The Dutch discover New Belgium (New York, 1609)— The Puritans build Boston (1630)—Oxenstierna founds New Sweden on the Delaware (1638)—The English conquer New Belgium (1664)— Penn founds Pennsylvania (1682)—Oglethorpe founds Georgia (1732).

THE east coast of the United States, from Florida to Canada, is about 1600 geographical miles long. Parallel with the coast, in the same direction, runs a chain of mountains, the lines of which are six or seven times repeated, and are called the Alleghany, *i. e.* the endless mountain ranges. The district between these mountain

VOL. II.

CHAPTER IV.

THE MARCH OF THE RUSSIANS AND COSSACKS THROUGH SIBERIA TO AMERICA.

PAGE

Annika Stroganoff sends his People over the Ural (anno 1570) — Jermak Timofejeff and his Cossacks ride over the Ural (1578)— Jermak gains Possession of " Sibir" (1580)—The Cossacks reach the Lena (1628)—The Cossacks gain Possession of Kamtschatka (1690-1706)—The Cossacks hear of the "Great Land," (America) (1706) —Peter the Great orders the Discovery of the "Great Land," (North-West America) (1723) — Behring and Tschirokoff reach America from Siberia (1741)—The Russians take Possession of North-West America (1760) 144

CHAPTER V.

THE NORTH AND THE ENGLISH.

Martin Frobisher's Voyages to "Meta Incognita" (anno 1572-1578) —John Davis discovers Davis's Strait (1585)—Henry Hudson discovers Hudson's Bay (1610)—Bylot and Baffin discover Baffin's Bay (1616)—John Ross begins the Series of Arctic Expeditions of

CONCLUDING OBSERVATIONS ON THE RESULTS OF THE DISCOVERY OF AMERICA TO COMMERCE, NAVIGATION, SCIENCE, RELIGION, AND POLITICS.

Introduction of European Diseases—Changes in the Condition and Habits of the Natives of America—Destruction of the American Civilisation—Extinction of the Red Race—Development of New Races — Changes in the Aspect of Nature, and in the Climate through the Cultivation of the Soil and the Introduction of New Animals and Plants: Sugar, Coffee, Cotton, Negro Slavery—Spread of American Plants and Animals in Europe: Potatoes, Tobacco, Maize, Medicines, Turkeys—Changes of Political and Commercial Power and Hegemony in Europe— Zenith of the Power of the Portuguese and Spaniards, and its Decline—Decline of Italian Commerce; of German Commerce; of the Hanse Towns—Freedom of the Netherlands — Rise of the English — Influence on Sciences— Cosmology—Astronomy — Botanical Gardens — Menageries — Natural Sciences—Ethnography—History of Man—Impulse to Invention—Increased Moral and Physical Mobility of European Nations —Modern Languages and Literature—Spread and Stability of the Christian Religion 231

A POPULAR HISTORY

OF THE

DISCOVERY OF AMERICA.

―――♦―――

CHAPTER I.

THE NAVAL HEROES OF QUEEN ELIZABETH, AND THE EAST COAST OF THE UNITED STATES.

John Cabot discovers North America (June 24, anno 1497)—Ponce de Leon discovers Florida (1513)—Coligny's Huguenots in Florida (1562, 1568)—Sir John Hawkins's Expeditions (1562, 1565, 1567)—Sir Francis Drake's Voyage round the World (1577, 1578)—Sir Humphrey Gilbert's first Attempt at Colonisation (1583)—Sir Walter Raleigh's Voyage to Virginia (1584 and 1602)—John Smith Colonises the Bay of Chesapeake (1607)—The Dutch discover New Belgium (New York, 1609)—The Puritans build Boston (1630)—Oxenstierna founds New Sweden on the Delaware (1638)—The English conquer New Belgium (1664)—Penn founds Pennsylvania (1682)—Oglethorpe founds Georgia (1732).

THE east coast of the United States, from Florida to Canada, is about 1600 geographical miles long. Parallel with the coast, in the same direction, runs a chain of mountains, the lines of which are six or seven times repeated, and are called the Alleghany, *i. e.* the endless mountain ranges. The district between these mountain

VOL. II.

walls and the coast line is a beautiful strip of land 200 to 350 geographical miles broad, called by the Americans "the slope of the Atlantic," because its numerous rivers all flow into that ocean.

This Atlantic slope is at the present day by far the most important portion of America. Along its shores now lie the largest and most flourishing commercial cities, and more important interests and hopes are bound up in it than in any other part of the American coast of the same extent.

Like Central Europe, towards which its face is turned, it runs through the whole of the temperate zone. Its climate greatly resembles that of the best portions of our continent, whose natural productions and inhabitants flourish in it to great advantage.

Columbus gave to tropical America, which he discovered, the name of Western India. The north-west of the New World (the countries round Hudson's Bay) has been called American Siberia, and the north coast (Greenland and Labrador) the American Scandinavia. The east coast, with its adjacent countries, might with justice be called the American, or New, Europe. To Englishmen belongs the merit of having recognised the importance of this region; of having maintained their ideas respecting it, and having finally brought them to a fortunate issue.

They were the first to prove the existence of this coast, and to display their sails and pennants along its shores. This took place very soon after Columbus's first voyage, and before the close of the fifteenth century, in the reign of Henry VII.

Columbus had made known his projects and ideas to this king by sending to him his brother Bartholomew, and offering (though vainly) to undertake for him the work of discovery in the West. Thus he had been the first to awaken in the king a desire after the transatlantic world.

Henry VII., stung with vexation at the opportunity he had lost, set to work to gain a share in the prospects now opened in the West. A few years after Columbus's first voyage across the ocean, he despatched an exploring fleet in that direction, which, in the dearth of skilful English navigators, was commanded, like almost all the earlier expeditions of Europeans, by an Italian, the Venetian Giovanni Cabot.

To keep out of the way of the Spaniards, and for other reasons, Cabot did not turn to the South, but sailed across the ocean in a north-westerly direction, and discovered the great island of Newfoundland, with its abundant fish-banks, and on the 24th June (in the same year), on St. John's Day, the continent of North America, part of the present Labrador. He sailed down along the coast southward until, as he said, he thought himself in the same degree of latitude as the straits of Gibraltar; that is, nearly as far as the boundary of the present state of North Carolina, and then he returned to England. Thus he had seen the principal part of that wild and barbarous coast in which the English subsequently played so great a part.

Had the importance of Cabot's discovery been understood at that time, and the requisite means for prosecuting it been at command, this discovery might have been called sufficiently great; but wild coast-lands, which must be cultivated with the sweat of their brows, were not at all to the taste of the English.

They, like the Spaniards and all their contemporaries, wanted to find vast realms abounding in wealth, in splendid castles, and cities with which a profitable commerce might at once be set on foot.

The precise nature of the land they had seen was unknown to Cabot and his Englishmen. They, like Columbus, thought it was a part of Asia—the northern and eastern points of that northern Tartary which they believed stretched out far towards Europe.

In the oldest maps of the world which we still possess, Labrador, Newfoundland, &c., are represented as connected with Asia, something like the peninsulas of Kamschatka and Corea.

It is not surprising that in England the rejoicings over this discovery were not great, and that the English, who at that time possessed neither a superabundance of inhabitants nor a navy of any importance, should not immediately seize these paltry countries, which they rather looked upon as in the way of their plans. Nor need it excite our astonishment that Cabot had no successor; that his soon almost forgotten voyage should remain isolated, and that nearly a century should elapse before the English called their old Cabot and his voyage —then become famous—to remembrance, that they might found on it their right of discovery and their claim to the country.

The only immediate practical result of this discovery proceeded from the knowledge of the rich fisheries on the banks of Newfoundland, which, soon after Cabot's expedition, were visited and made profitable by European fishermen; though here, also, the English at first allowed other nations, especially the French, to take the lead.

The north coast of the United States is indicated in the oldest maps of the world by rough and uncertain strokes, as if a cloud or a mass of rocks was intended to be represented, and the vague inscription is appended, "Here land has been seen by the English." At the southernmost point the busy little coral insects—working from antediluvian times—have added a supplement to the

Atlantic slope, have built up a large and marvellous peninsula, four hundred miles in length. This reaches nearly to the tropical zone and to the Antillas Islands, possessed by the Spaniards; and it may have served as a primæval bridge for the migrations of the ancient American tribes. Now, the Spaniards could not help knowing, through their islanders, of this country to the north of Cuba. After their fashion, the Indians spoke of many strange and fabulous things in it, among others of a far-famed "Fountain of Bimini," which cured the sick and caused the old to become young again.

Sixteen years after Cabot, the Spaniard Ponce de Leon, Governor of Porto Rico, sailed to the north, to seek the "wonderful country of the well of life and the spring of youth, Bimini." He discovered this land on an Easter Sunday, which day is commonly called by the Spaniards "*Pascua Florida*" (the Festival of Flowers), and on this account, as well as because the country lay before his eyes decked in all the full beauty and fragrance of its spring flowers, he called it "*La Florida*" (the Island of Flowers). Ponce de Leon sailed round it, and several Spanish navigators followed in his track, continuing his discoveries on the west as well as the east side of the coral peninsula.

As early as the year 1525 the Spaniards had sailed along the whole coast of the United States, from Newfoundland to Cuba, and had taken possession of it for their king, in so far, at least, as such ceremonies as the putting up of crosses and coats of arms, cutting the king's name on trees, drinking sea-water, and waving flags could make it their own. They had, moreover, already given names to the principal capes, harbours, and bays of this coast. They called, for example, New York and the Hudson River, "the Harbour of St. Antonio;" our Chesapeake Bay, near which lies Baltimore, "the Bay of the Virgin Mary;" and the river of our present Philadelphia they named "the Bay of St. Christopher." The name of Florida, originally only applied to a part of the country, was soon extended by the Spaniards to the whole of the territory of the present United States, and they continued to call it thus for two hundred years. It is a pity that this pretty name has not been retained for the whole country, for then the citizens of the United States, whom a geographer scarcely knows how to designate briefly, would have had one proper name for both land and people. Those citizens who believe that "decrepid Europe," as they call it, becomes rejuvenated in their country, might then, likewise, have appealed to the historical fable of the "Well of Youth" as a pretty and very significant prophecy. These Spanish names, which were paraded on the maps of the world, remained, however, only empty words, out of which nothing grew—no colonies, no emporiums, no well-organised provinces.

The Spaniards were certainly jealous enough concerning everything in the half of the world which they had received from the Pope, and, as long as they could, they tried to stop foreigners from entering upon the wild eastern coast of America. But they did not see why they should build and plant in the north as long as they could reap, without sowing, in the south.

The east coast lay fallow, as it were, till the middle of the sixteenth century. As it promised neither gold, nor silver, nor spices, it was only of necessity, when nothing else was left, that people were driven to it. It was not a country which could enrich the crowns of kings with brilliants and pearls. It was a country for exiles, for the banished, and it is only by degrees that this despised land has become the corner-stone of the continent. The first fugitives, who sought not an empire to plunder, but rather a piece of earth to cultivate and live upon in freedom, came to this east coast from France, about the time of the wars of the Reformation.

On the extension of the Reformation to France, from the beginning, its spread became connected with the maritime undertakings of the people of that country. It took root in especial in several of the French harbours, and La Rochelle, St. Malo, and other sea-ports, soon formed the chief bulwarks of the Huguenots. Their great and most zealous patron and leader, Coligny, was High Admiral of France under King Charles the Ninth, and it may have been that the Huguenots, from the first, cast their eyes across the ocean to the new country as the proper field for their new religion.

The French corsairs and freebooters, who, in the sixteenth century, swarmed in the tracks of the Spanish and Portuguese, were not unfrequently commanded by Huguenots, who probably felt but little scruple in warring against Catholic kings.

The first attempt at a Protestant colony in the new world was made by Admiral Coligny and his adherents in the year 1554. His aim was to reach the coast of Brazil and the beautiful bay of Rio Janeiro, which had long since been descried by French fleets in the track of the Portuguese. This attempt was, however, entirely frustrated. The French who were settled in the district, where later the imperial capital of Brazil has been built, fell into disunion and dissensions, and such of them as remained were driven from the beautiful bay of Rio Janeiro in the year 1560, by a fleet-of-war which the King of Portugal sent out against them.

Upon this, Coligny turned his thoughts to the coast of Florida, which was not occupied by the Spaniards, and he sent thither many Protestant naval heroes in the name of the king. These men explored the coast more carefully than it had hitherto been done, and they built a couple of forts, which they maintained for some years against famine and the native tribes. From their forts they likewise penetrated into the interior of the country, following the course of the rivers. These excursions were made in the territory of the present states of South Carolina, Georgia, and Florida, which were the first lands explored by the French. They drew maps and inviting pictures of this attractive country, which found their way to France, were there printed, and afterwards translated and published in England.

This Huguenot colony, which they called " *la Floride Française*," was the first positive settlement which had been made by Europeans in the countries of the United States, and also the first plan of colonisation of the same nature as those which England afterwards so frequently carried out. Unfortunately, it came to a most tragical end. The Huguenots received but little support from the Catholic king, Charles the Ninth; the King of Spain, therefore, sent a superior fleet and army to take them by surprise. All those who did not fall defending themselves were taken prisoners (men and women) and at once executed, or rather murdered. The Spanish admiral, Menendez, who ordered this horrible butchery, caused a monument to be erected on the place of execution, where the victims still lay on the ground, or hung on trees, and on this monument he had the words engraved, "This befel them not as Frenchmen, but as heretics."

The Nemesis, however, soon followed; for, as King Charles the Ninth of France took no notice of this atrocious affair, a French nobleman, Gourgues, fitted out a fleet at his own expense, and falling as unexpectedly on the garrisons which the Spaniards had left in Florida, he took them prisoners and put them all to the sword; and, instead of the Spanish monument, he raised a French one, on which was inscribed, "This befel them not as Spaniards, but as murderers."

The French Protestant project of exploring and colonising the east coast now fell to the ground, for troublous times came for the Huguenots. Admiral Coligny and his followers, in that night of terror called the "Feast of Blood," suffered the same kind of death at the hands of their own king as the King of Spain had inflicted on their sea-captains and colonists in America. The discoveries they had made on the other side of the ocean continued to exist only in the papers and maps which they left behind them, and these coming afterwards into the possession of the English, were, in many ways, turned to good account by them in all their undertakings.

It is one of the most interesting tasks in the history of

discovery and of geographical science, as in that of all human knowledge, to trace out how the ideas are communicated by inheritance from individual to individual, and from nation to nation; to see how, and under what circumstances, one people, so to speak, inoculates another; how the impulse once given works on through races, and from neighbour to neighbour; and how, as one man retires from the arena, his successor takes the torch from his hand and carries its light still farther.

The English, in the greatest work which they have accomplished in America, the exploration and colonisation of the United States, have, in many cases, been the scholars and successors of the French. The accounts which the latter gave of the beauty and fertility of this region, and its fitness for man to dwell on, of its abundant harbours and rivers, and its temperate European-like climate, first kindled the desire of the English for the undertaking. They not only received this intelligence by means of the printing-press, but also by word of mouth; for many of the French fugitives and Huguenots came in person from Florida to England, where they were presented to Queen Elizabeth. These Frenchmen, too, who, at that time, were far better acquainted with the Atlantic Ocean than the English, frequently served them as pilots and steersmen in their voyages to the west. I could here give particulars to show how the English, in their earliest distant voyages, were always very desirous of having some of these French pilots on board their ships.

Even the famous statesman, Sir Walter Raleigh, who afterwards did so much for the east coast of America, received his inspiration from the French. In his youth he fought on the side of the Huguenots, and it is probable that he made the acquaintance of Admiral Coligny, whose life and deeds so much resemble his own.

Previous to the reign of Queen Elizabeth, the English had taken but little part in the transatlantic expeditions. At the period when the discoveries of the Spaniards and Portuguese most flourished, England, for forty years, was ruled by a narrow-minded despot, who, principally occupied with domestic affairs and internal dissensions, was little suited to inspire his subjects with a lively spirit of enterprise. The maritime trade of England was also, at that time, for the most part in the hands of the Hanseatic merchants, and England had neither so important a merchant service nor a navy as the Spaniards, or even as the French, had long possessed. All that Henry VIII. could do was to free the commerce of his country from dependence on foreigners, and lay the foundation of a future navy.

Even in the period following the death of this despot, though the navy gradually increased, yet the condition of the country was little favourable to great enterprises. Many rulers followed each other in rapid succession, and just at the time when the French, as the declared enemies of Spain, were busy in forwarding the work of discovery in America, the Queen of England, by a marriage with Philip II., prevented the English from coming forward as discoverers or conquerors on a continent which the King of Spain considered to belong to him from one end to the other. Such opportunities were only opened to them when they, like the French, became the declared enemies of the possessors of the new world.

This salutary change, this enmity, the English owed to their anti-Catholic queen, Elizabeth, whose reign commenced in 1558. Under this energetic and popular princess, the long-checked energies of the people, that had been gradually though silently preparing for action, suddenly burst forth, and she it was, also, who fostered the youthful efforts of the nation in navigation and discovery. She it was who built England's wooden walls; the gracious queen, like Peter the Great, often busying herself personally with their construction. She went herself on board the newly built ships, shook their rough captains by the hand, and drank with them a cup at parting. She consecrated their flags, and she, the Maiden Queen, stood on the balcony of her palace at Greenwich, amidst the thunder of cannon, when her sea-captains sailed past, waving her handkerchief to them as a sign of good wishes.

If they returned victorious, with her own hands she hung chains of gold round their necks, and knighted them. She thus inspired them with self-sacrificing zeal and heroism, and many a British seaman in foreign lands, when surrounded by difficulties and dangers, found, in his enthusiasm for his energetic maiden queen, new strength and courage. In this respect, they resembled Columbus, to whom the thoughts of his gentle queen Isabella always gave support.

The first naval hero of Elizabeth's time of any importance, of whom it can be said that he placed himself at the head of the movement, is Sir John Hawkins. He might be called the English discoverer of the West Indies, or the British Columbus. His life, his first attempts, and his final successes, present, in many respects, parallels to the life of Columbus, and to his trials and experiences. It is curious to remark how almost all the seafaring nations who took part in the discovery of America, each in its turn has passed, step by step, through the same phases as the Spaniards.

The French, the British, and the Dutch, each accomplished their own discovery of America after the example of the Spaniards. They each found their way first to the Azores, to the Canary Islands, and then to the Antilles, and thence further.

Hawkins, too, began with small voyages to the Canary Islands, and there he made zealous inquiries about the condition of the West Indian Islands. In 1562, from the Canaries he crossed the ocean, in the old route of Columbus, by the aid of the trade winds, and, like him, too, he returned by way of the Azores to England. In a second voyage, in 1565, he extended the field of his operations, and, again like Columbus, he sailed into the middle of the Central American Archipelago, made his way through all the Spanish possessions round Cuba, and reached the coast of Florida at a time when it was still occupied by the French Protestants. He was the first Englishman who conferred with them, and gathered from them a knowledge of the condition and advantages of the country; and he was likewise the first to convey such knowledge to England and spread it abroad.

These reports, which he brought home were, to be sure, very exaggerated, but they were naturally on that account only the more attractive to the English. The east coast of America was described as a second Eden; myrrh, frankincense, storax, gums and spices, of course were there in abundance; and, moreover, gold, pearls, and silver; and scarcely any of the creatures of Paradise were said to be wanting, not even the unicorn.

"For," said the reporter to Hawkins's expedition, "as it is proved that there are lions and tigers in this country and that nature invariably follows the rule of placing inimical races of animals together—the dog near the cat, the falcon near the sparrow, and the rhinoceros near the elephant—so it is evident that the unicorn, the deadly enemy of lions and tigers, must be found in North America." "And one may suppose," he continues, "that in a land which contains the veritable unicorn, many other prodigies and treasures may be discovered, all of which, with God's help, time will yet disclose to us."

By means of similar arguments and reports the English were allured to the country, which subsequently became famous for their colonisation.

A succession of naval heroes followed on the track of Hawkins, as they had done on that of Columbus. These expeditions resembled each other in a great degree in respect to their line of route as well as in the objects to be gained. They generally went straight from England to the Canary Islands, and thence to the coast of Africa. Here they hunted down negroes, and filling their ships with a cargo of these wretched slaves, so welcome to the Spanish colonists, and avoiding the Spanish fleets on reaching the West Indies, they sold their slaves, or with threats they forced them on the planters for whatever price they chose to give. After this they pursued the Spanish ships, and if they found themselves strong enough for an attack, they lay in wait for the royal silver fleets, and they generally returned to Europe, laden with plunder, through the West Indian Gibraltar, the Straits of Florida.

As the age of the Portuguese and Spanish heroes was already past, the youthful English navy gained ground with great rapidity. It soon was seen in the South Atlantic Ocean, and, in the year 1577, the English Magellan entered upon the scene.

Sir Francis Drake, the first Englishman who sailed round the world, again found the straits that had been discovered by Magellan: He unfurled the English flag in the Pacific Ocean, and sailed round the whole of the great continent of America as far as California, which he called New Albion, going up much farther to the north than any Spaniard had done before him. The American discoveries made by Hawkins, Drake, and their contemporaries were partly re-discoveries of tracts of land which the Spaniards had already begun to neglect; they were, however, in many cases, disclosures of regions never seen before. They burst upon the whole Spanish possessions like a tempest, and, like it, more destructively than beneficially. They overshot their mark, as is usually the case in the first vigour and pride of youth. Like the Spaniards themselves, who had begun in the new world by plundering the Aztecs and Incas before they founded new settlements, the English first begun by plundering the Spaniards in the hemisphere belonging to them; and their easy conquest caused them to overlook things of much greater importance. More than twenty years of Elizabeth's reign were consumed before any one thought of establishing a solid, useful, permanent, and agricultural settlement.

Such an idea was first fully and clearly developed in the minds of two brothers—Sir Humphrey Gilbert and Sir Walter Raleigh—one of whom met with his death in attempting its realisation, whilst the other, during his whole life, made the most strenuous efforts in the cause. Both were born in the family and on the estate of a country gentleman, in the western extremity of Southern England, where, from childhood, the ocean had worked upon their young imaginations and influenced their boyish sports. Both made themselves acquainted, by diligent study, with the history of that ocean; in other words, with the history of the Spanish discoveries in America; and both perceived in which direction the largest field for English colonisation and conquest was to be found.

When they attained the age of manhood, they both of

them wrote down their views on this subject, and published them. The elder brother, Sir Humphrey Gilbert, succeeded at last in gaining the support of the Queen, who sanctioned his undertaking, and gave him a small fleet. This was the first fleet which ever left the shores of England not freighted with over-rapacious, slave-hunting men, but with workmen, handicraftsmen, miners, engineers, and scholars—the true seed for a colony.

Their destination was the barren east coast of the country which had been so attractively described by the French, and was still called Florida. Sir Humphrey proposed to reach it on the northern track by way of the banks of Newfoundland, and not by the Spanish course through the Antilles. Unfortunately, he did not get much beyond these banks. His largest vessel went to pieces on the coast of that desolate island, Nova Scotia, and all the elements of colonisation were scattered on its beach. This island, so celebrated for shipwrecks, was called by the English "Sable Island."

Sir Humphrey Gilbert himself, however, in attempting to return to England with the remainder of his followers in two small vessels, was overtaken by a storm in the middle of the ocean, and swallowed up by the waves. It was in this storm, and shortly before he sank for ever, that he called out to his terrified companions, "Brothers! be consoled, we are as near Heaven on the sea as on shore." These memorable words have become proverbial in the English navy.

I may here remark that many of the pithy and striking sayings current amongst English seamen were first pronounced by the naval heroes of Queen Elizabeth's time on their expeditions to America.

Only one small vessel returned to England with the news of the destruction of the father of the project of colonisation in North America.

But the brother of Sir Humphrey Gilbert, the much more celebrated Sir Walter Raleigh, the knightly lover and powerful favourite of Queen Elizabeth, prevented the plans of his shipwrecked brother from falling to the ground. He it was who steadfastly supported every naval enterprise, and he may well be called the Coligny of England. For a long course of years he employed all his energies, his influence with the queen, and his capital, which had been greatly increased by the queen's bounty, in the furtherance of these plans.

Year after year Raleigh equipped and sent forth so many small fleets to the east coast of America in the cause of exploration and colonisation, that the English poet Spencer, in one of his odes, gave him the title of "The Shepherd of the Ocean."

His captains discovered in especial that portion of the coast which now belongs to North Carolina. And in the great bays and sounds of this coast, which we at present call the Sounds of Pamlico and Albemarle, on a little island called Roanoke, the first English colony in America was founded, and called the City of Sir Walter Raleigh. From this basis the surrounding country, with its rivers, inlets, and harbours, was carefully explored.

Their descriptions of this region, like all the first descriptions of the discoverers in America, were in the highest degree inviting. It seemed as if a paradise had been discovered.

The maiden Queen of England, at whose feet Raleigh laid this Eden, never yet trodden by the foot of greedy Spaniard, and inhabited only by the children of nature, called it Virginia—the virgin land—and she bestowed it upon her beloved Raleigh, that he might explore, conquer, colonise, and govern it.

The name Virginia was soon extended to the whole east coast, to the north as far as Newfoundland, and to the south to the peninsula of Florida; for the queen and Raleigh claimed this whole extent of country (although they only knew one part of it) as belonging to the English since the time of Cabot.

It is to be regretted that this beautiful name of Virginia, which recals many flattering hopes and pleasant circumstances connected with its origin, has not continued to designate the whole of the United States, instead of a limited portion of them only. It would have suited those who love to call their native land "a virgin country"—and who, in many respects, have aright to do so—even better than the name of Florida.

The progress of the English in this virgin country was, however, very slow. Neither Raleigh nor Elizabeth gained any advantage whatever from their costly efforts, their fine inventions, and their colonial settlements. Before the daughter-country could be established the mother-country had to defend herself against an attack of the Spaniards which threatened her destruction. King Philip prepared his great Armada to conquer the British Islands, and thus at once to put an end to the source of so much mischief to his possessions in America.

The queen was obliged to call in her Drakes, her Frobishers, her Grenvilles, and other sea-heroes, from all parts of the ocean; and, by the help of these brave men and an opportune storm, the naval forces of the Spaniards were dispersed. But, after this, such a rage for capturing or destroying the ships, harbours, and colonies of the enemy seized the English navigators, who followed close on the heels of the Spaniards, that for the remainder of the century, and Elizabeth's reign, the peaceful colony of Virginia was entirely forgotten. In the midst of all these storms, however, Raleigh himself constantly thought of the city on the Roanoke, named after himself; but it was difficult for him to collect money for new equipments and the succours so much required.

Shipowners and capitalists found it much more advantageous to fit out privateers to bring back richly-laden Spanish galleons than to invest their money in the purchase of agricultural implements, cattle, and seeds, which only after the lapse of years could return interest for the outlay. Even the commanders and crews of the new expeditions which Raleigh managed to fit out and send off, together with the emigrants, either changed their minds on the way, or at sight of the desolate coast of North America, and, carried away by the universal passion, they degenerated into pirates, turned their helms about, and sailed to the south to take part in the chase of the Spanish silver galleons.

His colonists and pioneers in Virginia were consequently destroyed by hunger, by want of every kind, and by the attacks of the now irritated natives. Twenty years later it was found out that in a general revolt of the Indians all the colonists had been slain, just as the Huguenots of Coligny had been destroyed by the Spaniards.

The end of both these great men resembled the fate of their colonies: Coligny was murdered by his king because he was a Protestant, and Raleigh's monarch,

James I., brought him to the scaffold on the pretext of his being a traitor. Notwithstanding that in the beginning of the seventeenth century Raleigh's Virginia was but an empty name, a barbarous uninhabited coast, strewn with wrecks and the bodies of European colonists, yet he had not lived or striven for it in vain. His own and his brother's projects of colonisation had been imparted to many minds. He had awakened in his native land a general interest for such schemes destined to be displayed as soon as the storms and the war-fever against Spain should become somewhat abated.

If the seeds which he had planted in the new world had not come to maturity, yet his ideas had taken root in the old, and were ready to put forth fresh buds under favourable circumstances. The English have been repeatedly praised for their capacity for exploring and colonising new countries. No one would wish to deny them this aptitude, but it must at least be acknowledged that they attained it very slowly, and after many unlucky attempts; more gradually, indeed, than other nations. The first Spanish colony which Columbus founded at Hayti had certainly as unfortunate a fate as almost any of the first settlements of the Europeans in America. But in the following year the Spaniards at once founded new colonies, which soon so increased in prosperity, making such constant progress that there never could be any idea of their being abandoned. Thirty years after the landing of Columbus, Hayti, Cuba, and other countries of the West Indies, abounded not only in mines and pearl-fisheries, but in settlements, gardens, sugar plantations, pasturages, and a number of small but promising towns.

One hundred and thirteen years after the first voyages of their Cabot along the coast of the United States, and forty years after their queen had given to the country the name of Virginia, the undertakings of the English on the coast often hung by a thread, and were frequently on the point of being abandoned. And from this date more than two hundred years had to pass over before any considerable advance into the interior of the country was made.

The discoveries of the Spanish and Portuguese, when compared to the progress made by the English, are like the flight of an eagle.

In regard to the latter, however, with greater justice might be applied the words of our poet, Schlegel, on the growth of the Roman empire:

> "But Lavinium was first founded, then Alba,
> Of Rome, no mortal yet had heard;
> Its birth dawned slowly into light,
> No greater ere was seen. The fates strove all they could."

Besides the causes already adduced, this tardiness and

the whole peculiarly piecemeal development of the English power on the east coast were partly owing to the natural conditions and the original political state of this region. The extension of the Spanish dominion was, as I have said, often rendered easy by the fact that they here and there found states of great extent ready organised, and when once they obtained possession of their rulers and the centres of their power, their sway immediately became equally great.

The English, on the other hand, found on their east coast a multitude of small and disunited savage tribes, whose different languages and customs they were obliged to learn, and with whom they had to wage a guerilla warfare—regular campaigns or expeditions not being possible.

The Spaniards, moreover, on the Orinoco and the La Plata, and the French on the St. Lawrence and the Mississippi, met with vast navigable rivers, which, when they had been once discovered, forthwith opened a way for hundreds of miles into the interior. The discoverer, who reached the mouth of one such river, sailed immediately upwards gaining with one blow an empire.

On the east coast of the United States, there were no such noble far-extending rivers. This coast is, as it were, divided by nature into small parcels. There were innumerable small rivers, which, at a little distance from the coast, are partly broken up by cataracts. Everywhere there are small bays, inlets, and harbours, one seeming to be as good as another, and no one fitted to attract attention by its great superiority; as, for example, the Bay of Guayaquil on the coast of Peru, or the estuary of the La Plata on the coast of Brazil. And not far from the coast, a sixfold barrier of rude thickly-wooded mountains extends.

The character of the coast-lands, so broken up and separated from one another, rendered them little suited to be taken possession of by any monarch or heroical adventurer. They were, so to say, organised by Nature for a republic; and, like the detached valleys of Switzerland, they were favourable to the establishment of many little communities, which communities, however, could only take root along the coast, and had to gain strength and to become united before they could break through the barrier which cut them off from the interior. Accordingly, in the course of the seventeenth century, we see a succession of expeditions, often consisting of but a few vessels, sometimes of one ship only, go forth laden with discoverers and colonists to settle—like swallows on the eaves of a long building—on one or other point of the coast. These floating cradles which were rocked across the ocean, carrying with them the germs of a new state, belonged for the most part to the

English, who first began the work, and who were finally destined to keep the whole for themselves. But other nations thronged to those parts of America likewise: the Dutch, Swedes, the Germans; indeed, all the branches of the Germanic race and of Protestant faith, whose desire for civil and religious liberty drove them to abandon their old homes.

It is not my business here to enter into all the interesting details of these most remarkable and eventful American expeditions, their various motives and aims; but, in so far as necessary to the completion of the history of discovery in America, I must call the attention of the reader to the principal points as tersely as possible, and, as nearly as I can, in chronological order.

The first solid, and in the end successful, colony (though often near to destruction), was established by the English at the entrance of that combination of harbours, inlets, and rivers, which we now call Chesapeake Bay.

The deep opening of this bay had been seen by the captains of Sir Walter Raleigh, and some London merchants and wealthy noblemen, soon after, established a company to form a settlement there. From the year 1606 this company dispatched many expeditions, and on the so-called King's River, a town was built and named Jamestown, in honour of James I.

For an entire century this town continued to be the capital of that part of the country called by the English "Southern Virginia." Soon after the establishment of this colony, one of the emigrants, John Smith, took the lead in its affairs, and by his energy and statesman-like wisdom he saved it from ruin. He was, also, the most active explorer of the neighbourhood. In a small boat, accompanied by a few English noblemen and seamen, he sailed up and sounded all the innumerable creeks, rivers, and harbours of that incomparable bay which extends inland for upwards of four hundred miles. He gave them the geographical names which they bear to this day, made a map of them, which one hundred years later, was the best of its kind; and he described them in writings, of which thousands of copies were distributed all over England.

This governor, John Smith, is looked upon as the father of the present State of Virginia, whose great arteries all converge towards this bay. Jamestown and the waters of Chesapeake Bay forming, as it were, the nucleus of the State which by degrees grew up around them. It was he, too, who fixed upon, and drew upon the maps, those points around the bay on which the flourishing cities of Baltimore, Washington, Richmond, and Norfolk were built, and thus, in a certain way, he may be called their creator.

At the time when this took place in the south, a company of merchants and politicians was formed in the city of Plymouth, in the west of England, for the purpose of exploring and colonising the north portion of that long coast which was then called North Virginia, but which soon afterwards received the name of New England. For twelve years this company, year by year, sent out ships and men to the cold, rocky and sterile country without being able to bring about a permanent settlement, but they at least became acquainted with all the harbours, bays, and mouths of rivers, and spread this knowledge in England, thus encouraging voyages in that direction.

At length, in 1620, a handful of persecuted emigrants, driven more by accident than by design to this coast, succeeded in bringing about that which neither kings nor mercantile companies had been able to achieve. These were the hundred and two Puritans on board the ship "Mayflower"—which, like another Noah's Ark, has become celebrated in America—who in the new world sought an asylum from the persecutions of the Anglican Church. As they had been banished several years from their native country, and beating about, vainly seeking an undisputed "biding-place,"—which, even in Holland, had been denied them,—they called themselves "The Pilgrims."

These pilgrims clung to the rocks of the new land like shipwrecked and homeless men, driven by their great need as well as their stern resolve; at length they built "New Plymouth," the first permanent English city in the north, as Jamestown was in the south.

There, on the celebrated "Pilgrims' Rock," in the midst of all the evils which the American Pandora inflicted on all the first settlers, their little banner waved on high. As the oppression of the Nonconformists and Puritans still continued in the mother country, new wanderers followed soon on the footsteps of the "Pilgrim Fathers," and increased their numbers.

In the year 1628 a party came over who founded Salem, the second oldest city of New England, and two years after, a more numerous one followed, who built the present capital of the north of America, the rich city of Boston.

Soon afterwards, the Archbishop of Canterbury taking severe measures against the Puritans, they fled by thousands across the ocean to establish a church according to their own wishes, or, as they said, "according to the injunctions of the Bible," and to escape the edicts of faith and the dogmas of the king and his bishops.

The great bay of Massachusetts received them all, and, like Chesapeake Bay in the south, it became the cradle of all the future States, and the point whence all farther discoveries and conquests were undertaken.

The want of room and arable ground on the sea-coast was soon felt; the settlers began to explore the interior, to purchase new tracts of land from the Indians, and to push the settlements up the rivers discharging themselves into the bay. But more than to any other cause this extension was owing to the dissensions which broke out among the colonists. The Puritan, and often *ultra*-Puritan Pilgrim Fathers of Plymouth, Salem, and Boston, were far from conceding to others that freedom of faith and conscience which they had in vain demanded for themselves from the English bishops. They wished to maintain their Church and religion in their purity, and strictly in accordance to their own views and purposes, and in the spirit of intolerance they excommunicated all those members who refused implicitly to conform to all their favourite dogmas.

This gave rise to further migrations, to the dispersion of various parties over the country, to the discovery of new districts suitable for settlement, of convenient rivers and harbours; and thus new communities were founded, from which, at last, have sprung the present states of New England called Rhode Island, Connecticut, and New Hampshire, states which have long venerated the old town of Massachusetts on the bay as their parent colony.

This further dispersion and founding of new and

flourishing states was owing to circumstances similar to those which had originally led to the exploration and colonisation of the whole of New England. Religious differences were at the bottom, and the leaders of these branch colonies and exploring parties, which pressed onwards to the north and west, were, for the most part, schismatic ministers, whom the Puritans had banished.

As the descendants of their followers have increased like the sands of the sea, these state-founding preachers are now as much honoured by millions of people as Abraham or Jacob, Lycurgus or Solon.

It may be said that this peculiar spirit of Puritanism, associated, however, with other qualities of the restless and inflexible Anglo-Saxon race, still continues to work, and has called into life many new creations in the far west of America.

The northern and southern fields of English exploration and colonisation had for a long time no connexion with each other. They were separated by a broad strip of country not yet in the possession of the English, and not only were these two colonies fed by emigrants of a different character, but different ocean tracks led to them.

Virginia, even in Cromwell's time, was reached by the old Spanish southern course, by way of the Antilles, while to new England the voyage was by the north, across the banks of Newfoundland. The intermediate space was unknown to the English, and it was here that another European people, the Dutch, managed to fix themselves.

The war of England with the Spaniards in Elizabeth's time, and the first development of the English navy, were contemporary with the revolt of the Netherlands—a country which had equally broken with Rome—against the Spanish yoke; and the consequences of this revolt were the same, namely, an extraordinary flourishing of the navigation of the Low Countries, numerous voyages of discovery, and numerous transatlantic conquests.

These achievements of the Netherlanders they owe in part to their alliance with the English, and in part to following their example. Like the English, the Dutch sent forth corsairs, who swarmed round and pursued the Spanish squadrons, and, like the English, they rose from pirates to the position of naval heroes. With English and French adventurers in alliance, they made their appearance early in the southern part of the Atlantic Ocean. The great Dutch navigators of the ocean had frequently English and French pilots on board.

With similar motives to those which had first led the Spaniards and Portuguese, and indeed all maritime nations across the ocean, the Dutch were inspired by the longing for the treasures of the East; and at the end of the sixteenth century they founded their Oriental Company, which forthwith began to drive the Portuguese from one East Indian position after another.

Like their predecessors, the Dutch found America on their way to the East, and American interests grew to such importance in the beginning of the seventeenth century, that to their Eastern Company they added a Western, or rather West Indian, Company. For some time it appeared as if these two Dutch mercantile companies were destined to divide the world between them, just as the Pope had already divided and apportioned it to Portugal and Spain.

As the Spaniards under Magellan, and the English under Drake had done, the Dutch, too, sailed round the south of America into the Pacific Ocean, and here, under their captain, Le Maire, they discovered the extreme point of the continent, Cape Horn, so called after the little Dutch town of Hoorne.

On the way thither they began to inspect Brazil for themselves, and to make conquests there, driving away the Portuguese, at that time subjects of the King of Spain, as they had already done from the East Indies. Like the English, and almost contemporaneously with them, the Dutch at last turned their attention to the east coast of North America, and here discovered the most beautiful harbour, and the most important river of the whole Atlantic slope, which the English had till now overlooked. This memorable discovery was made in 1609, by a naval hero of Queen Elizabeth's time, Henry Hudson, who was in the service of the Dutch. This great navigator explored the coast for the Dutch, in parts which had continued unknown to his countrymen. The river which he found was the one that still bears his name, the beautiful river "Hudson" of New York. Of all the rivers and river valleys of the Atlantic slope, not one has such a world-spread importance as this. It is a wild mountain chasm filled with water, which, cutting far into the country, and running due north from the south, like a vast canal, is navigable to a point not far removed from the great river St. Lawrence, with which, however, it is brought into connexion by two branch rivers and valleys.

Hudson, after regaling the inquisitive inhabitants on the banks of the river with Dutch beer, sailed up the river for more than two hundred English miles, and observed how extremely well qualified it was for commerce and colonisation. This voyage was performed in his little vessel " The Half-Moon," which is as celebrated in New York at the present day, as the before mentioned " Mayflower" of the Pilgrim Fathers is in Boston, or as the "Victoria" of Magellan was once in Seville.

At the mouth of this river, on one of the most beautiful harbours of the coast, lying between the English colonies in the north and the south, the Dutch built their "New Amsterdam," and they founded there the North American province of "New Belgium," which flourished contemporaneously with Virginia and New England, and became the nucleus of the New York of the present day.

Scarcely had this Dutch settlement begun to flourish than ships freighted with European seeds and agricultural implements, with hands eager for work, and heads filled with Protestant ideas, came to the coast to seek an asylum. These ships, which came the beginning of the third decade of the seventeenth century, bore the Swedish flag, and they endeavoured to press in between the Dutch and the English at the mouth of the river where now the wide-spreading city of Philadelphia is situated. The great King Gustavus of Sweden and his chancellor, Oxenstierna, had, like all the northern Protestants, cast their eyes on North America, in order to open an asylum for their poor; and in especial for those Protestant Germans whom the Thirty Years' War had left in the most terrible state of destitution and oppression. To these they issued a very remarkable proclamation. The ships just alluded to, therefore, brought over Germans as well as Swedes, likewise Finns. They held on there for about twenty years, and their little communities and churches laid the basis of the present State f Delaware. But their neighbours, the Dutch, considered them usurpers and intruders, and they sent out, in the year 1655, their general, Stuyvesant, who brought New Sweden under the dominion of New Belgium. Not long afterwards, however, this flourishing New Belgium was looked upon as a usurpation, and swallowed up by the people of New England.

England, at first the ally of the Dutch, had at last taken arms against her neighbour, whose power increased so rapidly, and, under Cromwell, the two countries had become the bitterest enemies. In a series of wars and sanguinary engagements the power of the Dutch on the Atlantic Ocean was broken.

At the peace of 1654 they were obliged to acknowledge the superiority of the English.

In the same year they gave back all their Brazilian conquests to the Portuguese, who 'had meanwhile freed themselves from the yoke of the Spaniards, and ten years later they lost their New Belgium, together with the New Sweden which they had added to it.

Cromwell was the first who thought of taking it from them, and this intention was again entertained under his son, but the uncertain state of affairs in England at that time prevented it being fulfilled.

But when Charles II. had re-established the throne, internal peace prevailed; and after the discoverers and colonists from New England in the north, and from Virginia in the south, had approached from either side to the settlements of the Dutch, the time arrived for decisive measures, and, in 1664, without much bloodshed these broad districts on the Hudson and Delaware were taken possession of by an English fleet.

The Dutch were now driven out of almost all their American positions and entirely from the mainland. At this day they only retain two little West Indian islands and part of the coast of Guiana to do what they like with.

The Netherlands, however, in the flood-tide of its power and prosperity, produced the most learned geographers, naturalists, and the most correct and indefatigable designers of maps in Europe. Their historical, nautical, physical, and cosmographical works relating to the discoveries of this time, and particularly of the earliest history of America, are most important, and take rank next to those of the Spaniards. Moreover, in the State of New York, which the English established on Dutch foundations, the character and customs of that people have had considerable influence, traces of which may be observed at the present day.

The settlers in New Sweden, at the mouth of the Delaware, had not spread themselves far into the interior of the country. Even on this side the Alleghanies there were extensive land and river districts still unexplored, on which, however, not long after the English conquest, an Englishman, celebrated in the history of discovery and colonisation in North America, cast his eyes.

It was William Penn, and from him this country received its name of "Penn's-sylvan-land," or Pennsylvania. This Penn was a gentleman possessed of considerable property, the son of a distinguished admiral. He had early taken the greatest interest in the persecuted sect of the Quakers, and, inheriting from his father a claim on King Charles II. for 16,000*l*., he requested that monarch to give him, instead of the money, the above-mentioned woodlands of the Susquehanna and Delaware rivers.

Charles, who was often in difficulties, gave Penn and his Quaker followers possession of, and government over, the whole tract of land lying between 40 and 43 degrees of latitude west of the river Delaware, and, in 1682, the "Quaker-king" landed on the coasts of the new world, bringing with him, at once, not fewer than two thousand of his co-religionists, who, subsequently, spread all over the country. The Swedish and Dutch settlers still remaining in the country did homage to Penn as their feudal lord, and he took possession of the neighbouring country, fixed his capital at Coaquanock, a little place inhabited by Swedes and Indians, which was henceforth called "The Brother City," or Philadelphia. He made arrangements, too, with the Indians of the Delaware and Susquehanna, whereby they likewise gave up to him their original right to the land which the king had already bestowed upon him.

After this, he gave to his state such peculiar and humane laws, that, if the "pious experiment" had succeeded, and had not, in the end, been overthrown, it would have been one of the happiest and most Christian states which the world has ever seen.

Penn, "the great and good Miquon," as his Indians called him, was an unwearied traveller, and, before he went to America, had become acquainted with France and other parts of Europe. He undertook, too, many journeys of discovery in his American dominions; he explored almost the whole of the River Delaware, which he sailed up to a distance of about three hundred English miles from its mouth. He repeatedly made excursions into the territory of the Indians on the Susquehanna, and the world owes its first authentic intelligence and its comprehensive knowledge of these two rivers to the papers subsequently published by him.

The news that William Penn had opened a "new asylum for the poor, the good, and the oppressed of all nations," on the other side of the ocean, spread throughout Europe, and from Scotland and Ireland, from the Netherlands and the Rhine, where Penn himself had seen the great misery of the people—for just at this time France had made a wilderness of one of the most beautiful provinces of Germany—numbers hastened to the land of promise on the banks of the Delaware and Susquehanna. In the first instance they settled near the mouths of these rivers, and then near their falls, in the central parts of these watercourses; at length they migrated farther "backwards into the woods," as they expressed it.

In the beginning of the eighteenth century "the woods" were cleared further and further, the wild animals and the natives being driven farther to the west; at first as far as the celebrated "Blue Ridge," the most easterly chain of the Alleghanies, and which forms the horizon of the district surrounding the mouths of the Susquehanna and Delaware, but in the end they had to take refuge in the labyrinthine valleys of the mountains themselves. The Germans, who came in greater numbers to Pennsylvania (which was more an agricultural than a commercial state) than to any other of the coast-lands, and who filled many of the most beautiful districts with rich and prosperous villages, took a prominent part in the opening up of the Susquehanna.

The northern and central parts of the Atlantic coast, with their numerous bays and harbours, had, as we see, not only been made known as far as the foot of the Alleghanies, but filled with settlements—some of them flourishing towns—whilst in the south the coast lands continued to be a *terra incognita*. This was partly due to the singular nature of that country; the rivers which flow through it from the Alleghanies are not nearly so deep and navigable as the Hudson, the Delaware, or some other of those rivers which pour their waters into Chesapeake Bay. In the summer season, too, they are almost entirely dried up. The character of the coast, however, formed the greatest impediment. It is flat and sandy, and runs in long straight lines unbroken by bays.

From Florida to Chesapeake Bay there are no inviting harbours, there is no prominent cape behind which shelter can be found. Behind the long sand-banks and the succession of downs lie flat lagoons, and, further inland, extensive swamps. Near to the south shore of Chesapeake bay is the celebrated "dismal swamp," still further south comes the "great alligator swamp," and then, as far as Cape Florida, a complete series of marshy lands extending many hundreds of miles, and which it has not yet been possible to reclaim entirely. In the interior of the country are far-stretching deserts of sand, and, immediately behind them, equally extensive and monotonous forests of firs called the "Pine Barrens." A point not far removed from Cape Hatteras has gained a melancholy celebrity on account of the numerous shipwrecks which there have taken place, and Cape Fear and other promontories show by their names that they deserve no better reputation. There are, indeed, a few accessible harbours and bays, but for the most part they are not capable of receiving ships of the first class.

The first settlements which the French and English attempted in this neighbourhood in the sixteenth century —the one near to the then famous Port Royal, and the other in the neighbourhood of Roanoke, so often named above—made scarcely any progress, partly in consequence of the natural obstacles just enumerated.

For one hundred years afterwards, up to the end of the seventeenth century, these great coast-lands were still hidden in darkness and unknown. Their first explorers, the Spaniards, whose zeal for conquest and discovery had died out, kept them guarded by little garrisons in their old forts in the south as in former times, and they were glad to know that there was a great wilderness lying between them and the rapidly rising colonies of the English in the north. Not only the Spaniards, but the rest of Europe, knew this desert as far as Chesapeake Bay by the name of Florida only.

Here, too, as almost everywhere before the real work of discovery, conquest, and settlement was undertaken, small parties of adventurers acted as pioneers. And Virginia, like New England, became the mother of many branch states. The first wars with the savages had caused many small bands of Virginian planters to take flight, and these, driven into the woods, or putting to sea to seek a new country, landed, in 1622, on the coast of Carolina, in the same district where formerly the French Protestants and the earliest English settlers of Roanoke had located themselves. The first Virginian colonists collected round Albemarle Sound; they made journeys among the savages, and played among them, as an old historian describes it, "the part of Christian missionaries."

In the year 1653 the settlers in these lost and forgotten outposts were visited by an English gentleman, a Mr. Brigstock, and he wrote a description of the country, which was long considered the main source of information about it.

And soon afterwards, from New England, the seeds of new settlements were scattered in Carolina. The New England men roamed over the continent, as well as over the sea, to seek their fortunes. In the year 1660, a little barque, steered by these "New England men," appeared in the neighbourhood of Cape Fear. The adventurers disembarked, discovered the Cape Fear river, and bought from the natives a small piece of land on which they founded a little colony of agriculturists and herdsmen. Some colonists had come over, likewise, from the Bermuda Islands.

All these journeys, descriptions, and attempts at colonisation fixed the attention of the English on the south, and King Charles II., at the request of some lords and cavaliers, was induced in 1665 to bestow on the Duke of Albemarle and some other lords the whole of the territory of the "Virginian lakes" (the neighbourhood of Chesapeake bay), then occupied only by a few scattered settlers, as far as the Savannah river from the 36th to 31st degree of latitude, and extending westward from the Atlantic to the Pacific Ocean.

He gave them absolute proprietorship over this vast territory; power over life and limb; the right to appoint a governor; to make laws at pleasure; to let out all the royal fisheries, forests, and mines, and to call the land after his name, Carolina. What right Charles II. had to give away this country, says an English historian of that time, is not our affair to inquire. Suffice it to say the king did it, and the lords proprietors immediately sent over, to turn their deeds of presentation to account, a palatine with authority to appoint a governor.

One of their partners, the famous politician and philosopher, the Earl of Shaftesbury, was commissioned to draw up in proper form all the laws and regulations of a constitutional government. This was so well thought out, and so skilfully done, and instituted so many social ranks and interests to preserve the balance of power; and it either created or provided for the creation of so many great titles (palatines, admirals, chamberlains, landgraves, marshals, head constables, &c.), on paper, that a ready made empire, so to speak, was established as regards territory and written institutions at least, at a time when this new state possessed but a few hundred subjects.

From the year 1670 the first ships with settlers went over to this new Canaan. The first points that they sought and colonised were in the neighbourhood of the earliest of all the French settlements on the north in the districts around the great Sound of Albermarle, where also Roanoke lay; and in the south, near the bay of Port Royal and the "May river." Soon, however, another region lying between these two, the country around the mouths of the little rivers Ashley and Cooper, in consequence of its good pasturage and arable soil, was found the most attractive. And here the centre of Carolina was formed, and the city built, which, in honour of King Charles, was called "Charlestown," and which continues at the present day the largest and most populous city of the Atlantic slope. A governor, sent by one of these lords, took over the first citizens and plan of this city, which latter was as elaborate as the constitution of the state.

As entire tolerance and freedom for all religious sects was one of the first principles of the new state of Carolina, dissenters came from all parts of England and Scotland, and also from new England, where there was not liberty enough.

Dutchmen, too, came from New York dissatisfied with the conquest of New Belgium by the English, and at last there arrived many Huguenots from Languedoc. The little colony thus soon increased in numbers and extent.

Negotiations and wars with the Indians, and collisions with the neighbouring Spaniards, led to the first considerable expeditions into the interior. Very soon the natives were divided into the so-called Spanish and English Indians, fighting against each other with the help of their European patrons. The Spaniards, who longed to serve the English as they had served the French heretics in the same neighbourhood, attacked a Scotch settlement which had established itself at a distant southern outpost, and entirely destroyed it. To revenge this and other outrages, the English marched to the south in the beginning of the eighteenth century, with twelve hundred men under their then governor, Moor, of Charleston. They vainly besieged the Spanish city of St. Augustine, but on this occasion many planters saw, for the first time, those regions which subsequently formed the State of Georgia.

But long before this there must have been men in Carolina, who, for purposes of trade, rambled far into the interior. A Colonel Bull is mentioned at the end of the seventeenth century as " a great Indian trader."

Unfortunately, travellers of this kind have not left us any account of their discoveries. Probably they scarcely reached as far as the foot of the Alleghany mountains.

But expeditions of another and most detestable kind were likewise undertaken by the English, recalling the early Spanish times of horror; namely, excursions into the interior to hunt down and capture Indians to make them slaves. In the beginning of the eighteenth century it is related of a governor of Carolina, that he granted concessions and liberty to various persons to penetrate into the interior for the purpose of seizing as many Indians as they could, to bring them away, and sell them as slaves.

Among the colonists who in the beginning of the eighteenth century distinguished themselves by explorations in the west and towards the mountains, was a German Swiss, called Christopher Guffenried. He came in 1708 from Berne to America, landed in North Carolina, and he experienced many adventures and dangers on his way towards the west. A bold man, relying on his Swiss rifle, he fought his way through the unknown woods, and into the Indian land beyond the furthest settlements.

In the course of time, plague and small-pox diminished here, as elsewhere, the savage tribes, whilst the axes of the colonists cleared the woods and paved the way to the beautiful highlands of the Alleghanies.

Before these mountains, however, were ascended and crossed, one more branch state was developed in the south, and it extended to the extreme end of the eastern coast.

King Charles had contented himself, as I said, with the country as far as the river Savannah, which he had fixed on as the southern boundary to his province of Carolina. But to the south-west of this river there were other attractive rivers and valleys, those of the Altamaha, the Santilla, and the Apalachicola.

That the Spaniards did not now hasten to make the land which had been so often watered by the blood of their forefathers their own, was owing to their want of power. They stood still within the palisades of their little Augustino. England, however, with its internal troubles, was as unceasing in supplying men impatient of oppression and adversity, as she was fertile in the supply of aiding and creative minds. The colonists of Carolina, in the before-mentioned expeditions against the Spaniards and Indians, had, by repeatedly traversing the above-named river districts, become well acquainted with the land, and they pronounced it to be " the most beautiful country in the whole universe."

About the year 1730, an association of distressed Irishmen and persecuted Protestants was formed for the purpose of seeking a new asylum. One of the directors of this company, the famous General Oglethorpe, embarked in 1732 with a troop of colonists. He became the founder and lawgiver of an extensive new state in the southern part of North America, which received the name of Georgia, after the reigning king, George I. Oglethorpe was also the first who again explored and described this great district. He landed at the mouth of the great boundary river Savannah, sailed up it for some distance, and on its southern shore he fixed upon the most favourable spot for colonisation. It is on this very spot that Savannah, the populous capital of Georgia, has been built. Oglethorpe, the founder of Georgia, was a kind-hearted, energetic, and skilful leader, who won the hearts of the people, like Captain Smith, the founder of Virginia, or the Quaker Penn, " the star of Pennsylvania." His fame spread among the Indians, who formed alliances with him, giving him in the first instance all their territory to the south of the Savannah on the Ogeechee, on the Altamaha to the river St. Mary, and as far up these rivers as the flow of the tide. The St. Mary's river became the boundary between Georgia and Spanish Florida, and still separates these two states.

Not only did the fame of Oglethorpe and his country, Georgia, soon spread among the Indians of the Savannah, but likewise in the alpine valleys of the province of Salzburg, then greatly oppressed, and also in the Scotch

Highlands. Many British and German Protestants came over, and the country began even to be called "Southern New England."

Thus, as we have seen, towards the middle of the eighteenth century—by the two hundred years' labour of the English and their Protestant brothers; by means of the Huguenot Coligny, who was murdered in the cause; by the exploits of the "sea heroes" of Queen Elizabeth, who freed the ocean, along the coast, from the Spanish fleets of war; through the judicious efforts of Sir Humphrey Gilbert and Sir Walter Raleigh, who set colonisation before their countrymen as a labour of love; by means of the severity of King James and his bishops, who turned the Puritans into emigrants; through Cromwell, who drove the Cavaliers in great numbers from their castles into the wilderness; in consequence of the revolution of the Netherlands, which inspired the Dutch with ideas of governing the world; by means of the bloody tumults of the Thirty Years' War which drove out poor persecuted Germans and Swedes, and the dragonnades of Louis XIV., which compelled French Reformers to seek an asylum among the Indians—all the provinces of the eastern slope of North America were discovered and colonised. Then, as the small New Sweden was absorbed by the greater New Holland, and as this New Holland again experienced the same fate by the mightier England, till at last, the English overthrowing everything before them—driving out, in the northern New Scotland, the French, and, in the Southern Florida, the Spanish—the whole long chain of plantations became united under one head and blended into one nation.

And now colonisation and order prevailing along the coast-line, there came a time when, from this basis, the endless barrier of the mountains was to be overcome. The Alleghanies, almost uninhabited and covered with thick woods, had long remained a dark labyrinth, a fabulous *terra incognita* to the colonists. They called them the "Blue Mountains," because their points only appeared now and then in the clouds of the horizon. At first, as they had a very uncertain idea of the western extent of the continent, whose eastern coast they inhabited, they thought that the western base of these mountains was washed by the breakers of the South Sea.

Of the products, people, and animals, which were to be found in the labyrinthine valleys of these blue mountains, the most wonderful things were related. "I not only heard," writes a famous traveller in 1735, not much more than a hundred years ago, "of the extraordinary animals in those mountains, but I myself saw there elephants, the wildest horses, twice as large as our species of horses, and made like greyhounds in their hinder quarters. I saw oxen there, also, with ears like dogs, and another species of singular quadrupeds, greater than bears, and without a head or neck, and whose mouth and eyes nature, for security, had placed in the middle of the breast."

A very wonderful book might be written about the fabulous animals and monstrous creatures with which fancy, invention, or insufficient examination had peopled the woods of the new world; I say, also, "insufficient examination," for it is quite possible that any one, seeing a buffalo from a distance, with high shoulders and drooping head, sunk in the thick hair which covers his breast, might receive an impression of him similar to that given in the above description.

The idea that the waves of the South Sea washed the western base of the Blue Mountains must have been abandoned at the end of the seventeenth century, when the French discovered the Mississippi. After that it was seen that many long rivers flowed down from the western slope of the Alleghanies, and the English called them "the French waters." The knowledge of the "Far West," and of its magnificent plains spread among the inhabitants of the coast, and many of them came now and then to the tops of the mountains in order to look in that direction.

"On one of these mountains," so says an English colonial author of that time, "there is a spring called Herbert's Spring; from this the waters flow towards the west, and it is only removed a hundred steps from the farthest source of the rivers which flow into the Atlantic Ocean. Our people come very often to this spring to satisfy their thirst and curiosity, and in order to be able to relate afterwards that they have drunk of the French waters. Many of them only come as far as this point, and for a short time, but many remain longer, either charmed by the beauty of the surrounding scenery or from some other cause; and in consequence a saying is spread abroad that Herbert's well, from which the western plains can be seen, possesses magic properties, and that whoever drinks of its waters continues for seven years, unable to tear himself from the spot."

The inhabitants of the coast came so often to this enchanted Herbert's well, and to many similar spots, to look out towards the west, and to drink the French waters, that at last, after they had freed themselves from the English yoke, they were seized with a remarkable thirst for land, with a passionate desire for discovery and conquest.

Like a swelling stream which, here and there percolating its banks, finds other channels, so, first of all isolated adventurers, and then small bodies of men, and soon greater numbers, made their way over the wall of the Alleghanies. We know the histories and the names of all these adventurers, of these little troops of pilgrims journeying westward, and they are preserved as the first heroic pioneers of the west in the annals of the coast states, each of which contributes its portion.

This percolating process did not long continue; by the close of the eighteenth century the people swarmed across the Alleghanies, the boundary of the territory we have been considering, and since then their history has become a long triumphant procession, and the wearied eye scarce can count the conquests.

CHAPTER II.

THE FRENCH AND THE FUR-HUNTERS IN CANADA.

The Cabots discover the Fish-banks of Newfoundland (anno 1497)—Caspar de Cortereal discovers Labrador (1500)—Giovanni Verazano sails along the Coasts of North America (1524)—Jacques Cartier discovers the Gulf or St. Lawrence (1534)—Jacques Cartier discovers the River St. Lawrence and Canada (1535)—Roberval and Cartier go to Canada (1542)—Roberval and his Fleet disappear (1548)—Samuel Champlain founds Quebec (1608)—Samuel Champlain organises the Province of Canada, and explores the Lower Lakes (1608, 1635)—Father Mesnard discovers the Upper Lakes (1660)—The Jesuits Allouez and Marquette complete the exploration of Lake Superior and Lake Michigan (1666).

A GLANCE at the map of the world shows us that the Atlantic Ocean represents a broad valley, extending from pole to pole, and lying between the old and new worlds. There are two points in especial where this wide valley becomes comparatively narrow. One of them is in the south, between Africa and South America, where, from the latter continent, the peninsula of Brazil reaches out far towards the east. Of this narrowing of the ocean, I have already spoken, and shown how it was crossed by the Portuguese in the time of Columbus, who took possession of Brazil.

The other point where the ocean narrows is in the north, between France, Ireland, and North America. At this point the great continent stretches out its arms, so to speak—the hammer-shaped peninsula of Nova Scotia, and the broad triangular land of Labrador—towards Europe; and still further to the east there is the great island of Newfoundland with its moss-covered rocks.

Near Newfoundland, the warm waters of the Gulf stream, coming from the south-western tropical regions, meet with the cold currents from Baffin's Bay and the Greenland seas, which, as they flow from the north-east, bring with them icebergs laden with stones, earth, and other debris usually found on glaciers. At a point to the east of the above-named country, where these icebergs meet with the warm current of water, for countless centuries have they melted away, and the rocks and other débris which they have carried with them, have fallen to the bottom of the sea, helping to form that great submarine deposit which we now call the "Banks of Newfoundland."

These banks, like all others of the same character, are

the resort of innumerable shoals of fish, and under the surface of the sea they bring the soil and products of America somewhat nearer to Europe.

From this point to the nearest European countries, Iceland and Ireland, there is an open sea, from one thousand six hundred to two thousand miles wide; and as the remaining coast-line of America bends round far to the west, this point is plainly the most remarkable as regards a connexion between the Cis- and Trans-Atlantic worlds.

If at any point in pre-historical time America received inhabitants from Europe, this would seem to have been the most probable one. Here lies that "Helluland" (stone-land), and that "Markland" (wood-land) which I have already spoken of as fragments of America, and which, long before Columbus, had been reached and named by the Normans of old. This narrow part of the ocean, too, it is, which, in our days, has been found to be the most suitable for connecting the two great divisions of the earth with an electric wire.

No sooner had Columbus, and in his lifetime, turned the eyes and the sails of all the seafaring nations to the west, than this outstretching bastion of North America caught the attention of the captains of King Henry VII.; like as the bastion of Brazil had attracted the notice of the sailors of King Emanuel of Portugal.

The Portuguese came to the latter under their celebrated knight, Cortereal, on a voyage round the world, which they hoped to accomplish in this direction. They have left there nothing, however, beyond a few names which are still in use, and amongst which the name of the country, *Laborotors* (workmen), or "Labrador," is the best known. It was so named by the Portuguese, because they had caught there a few strong and well-built Indians, which raised in them the hope to find workmen as useful as those to be procured from their slave-coast of Africa.

To the outstretching northern lands the English, under the celebrated Cabots, had likewise come in the hope to meet with an open sea, and a northern passage round the world. The Cabots called the land "*Terra Nova*," or Newfoundland, a name which is now used only for an island. The Cabots brought back, too, the first news of the enormous shoals of fish on the banks of Newfoundland. These fish, they said, were called by the savage natives "*bacallaos*."

In consequence of the poor prospect that the circumnavigation of the globe could be accomplished by way of North America, the European monarchs soon ceased to send expeditions in that direction. But the inviting news of the fish-haunts in regions not so very far removed from Europe soon spread in the small fishing ports of

France and Spain, particularly in those of Normandy, Brittany, and Biscay.

In these harbours, from olden times, there lived a race of bold and experienced fishermen, accustomed to follow the whales and roving herrings far into the stormy Bay of Biscay. Scarcely had they heard of the fish "*bacallaos*" which, as already said, the Cabots had discovered, and which, they were told, appeared in such numbers on the banks of the new country that the ships actually stuck fast in them, than their fisher imaginations were just as much inflamed as those of the Spaniards about their El Dorados. They extended their fishing-grounds beyond the above-mentioned narrowing of the ocean, and made their appearance on those banks.

There came to them Portuguese and Spanish Biscayans; and, especially, very frequently the barques of the little seaports in Normandy and Brittany, Honfleur, Havre de Grace, Dieppe, St. Malo, La Rochelle, and the English soon followed.

This extraordinary fishery, which down to our times has played such an important part, and given rise to so many political disputes and negotiations, began in the lifetime of Columbus, and soon after his death there was scarcely any part of America, not excepting the Antilles, where European sails were more frequently seen than on the banks of Newfoundland.

The Indian name *bacallaos*, or *bacaillos*, or *bacalieu*, was introduced into the languages of all seafaring nations, and the fish themselves, salted and dried, found their way into the kettles of all good Christians. The fishermen of Lower Germany adopted the name, too, transforming it, however, into "*Kabeljau.*" It was even applied to the land which lay immediately behind those banks; and the wild coasts to which the seamen sometimes took refuge from storms, or to repair their vessels—those of Newfoundland, Nova Scotia, and Canada—were all classed together, and called "*la Terre des Morues,*" or "*Terra de Bacallaos.*" In fact, there exist old maps of America, on which the name "*Kabeljauland*" is given to a good portion of the country now belonging to the United States.

"*Kabeljau,*" or salted codfish, were the forerunners of the discovery of Canada, in like manner as spices, gold-mines, or other treasures of nature, had enticed Europeans to other parts of America. The French, who, in especial, as already said, profited by these fisheries, soon followed the retreating fish further to the western waters and the neighbouring coasts.

Indeed, not long after the Atlantic navigation had been opened by Columbus, the French took a very active part in the discovery of the new world. We find their enterprising seamen, who were constantly quarrelling with their neighbours on the other side of the Pyrenees, following the Spaniards in all directions. As freebooters and corsairs, they followed them to the Azores and Canary Isles, and, by the aid of the trade winds, to the Antilles. In the first years of the sixteenth century, too, before the Portuguese had settled in Brazil, the French appeared on the savage coasts of that land, and there cut logwood and loaded their vessels with it, as well as the Portuguese.

It is to be regretted that the earliest history of the French voyages across the ocean is so very obscure. We have no authentic information of the way in which they developed their marine, nor how they learnt the secrets of the Spaniards. The maps which they made of their discoveries are lost, and the names of their bold heroes, the contemporaries of Da Gama, Cabrel, and Magellan, are nowhere mentioned. In Spanish and Portuguese authors there appear occasionally only these "*Corsarios de Francia*," when they anywhere interfered with their people; when they burnt one of their towns in the Indies, or drove them from a silver mine; or when their monarchs found it necessary to send forth war fleets to the coast of Brazil, or elsewhere, to free the country of this plague. After such mention, they again escape us entirely, and even in the annals of their own country scarcely any mention of them is made.

The cause of this is plain enough. The kings of France, who had rejected the proposal of Columbus, and who, after the Papal partition of the world, had lost the proffered opportunity of gaining America for themselves, left everything in their country to private speculation. As long as they were at peace with Spain and Portugal, they had to appear to be ignorant of the bold ventures of private persons. Therefore, officially, no notice was taken of their most brilliant doings, nothing reported, and nothing written down. And the men of Brest, of Dieppe, and Rochelle, on their return, sold their booty, and enjoyed the profits as quietly as possible in their native seaports; and they related their adventures in the new world to their townsfolk only, by whose descendants all was forgotten.

In the northern districts of America, likewise, to which we are now giving our attention, everything was left to private speculation; and French fishermen long busied themselves in these waters, sailed about and made all kinds of discoveries, without either a monarch or any historiographer troubling himself about them.

All this was changed, however, when Francis I., the rival and enemy of Charles V., and who cared not for Spain, ascended the throne. This regenerator of arts and sciences took the navy under his royal protection, and promoted voyages for the discovery of distant lands.

In the year 1524 he sent vessels to America under the command of an Italian, Verrazano, who discovered for France the entire coast of the present United States. And again, in 1534, about the same time that Pizarro conquered the empire of the Incas for Charles V., the rival of Francis, the latter was persuaded by his admiral, Chabot, to send out two government ships under the command of Jacques Cartier, partly for the benefit of the sailors of Normandy and Brittany, to explore the countries lying behind their fisheries, and partly to see if a way could not be found between the islands by which to sail to China.

Cartier, the first discoverer of Canada and the St. Lawrence, made three extraordinary voyages to these regions. On his first voyage, he penetrated only into the great gulf which lies behind Newfoundland, of which the fishermen on the "banks" already knew something. The French Newfoundland voyagers called it simply "*la Grande Baie;*" the Spaniards, however, in consequence of its form, "*el Golfo Quadrado*" (the four-cornered gulf). It is now called the Gulf of St. Lawrence.

Cartier explored the bays and creeks in this gulf, in the hope of finding an outlet to the west, a passage to China and the Pacific. At length, he believed he had found one. He came to a strait in the background of which no more land could be seen, and the natives told him, moreover, that the water extended to the west without interruption. He named it the Strait of St. Peter (*Détroit de St. Pierre*). It was in reality the wide mouth of the river St. Lawrence.

The lower half of this river flows through a fissure six hundred geographical miles long, which runs in an almost straight line to the north-west. It has more the appearance of a colossal strait than of a river. It is everywhere broad, and it opens towards the sea like the end of a trumpet. To give an idea of the vast size of this river, it is sufficient to say that the tide, as far as Quebec, three hundred and fifty miles from its mouth, sometimes rises as much as twenty feet. Altogether the tide extends about as far up the river as the source of the Rhine is distant from its mouth. Whales and other sea monsters enter the river too, and ships can sail up its whole length.

When, therefore, Cartier looked into the mouth of the St. Lawrence, he took it for a marine channel, for a second Magellan's Strait. But, as autumn had now come, he was unable to penetrate farther, and he hastened back to France to bring Francis I. the joyful news; and the following year he was sent again, with more ships, to complete his discoveries. Cartier sailed direct to his " St. Peter's Strait," and as he ran into a small bay on St. Lawrence's day, he called it "*la Baie de St. Laurent."* From this little bay at its mouth the entire river, in the course of time, received its name. Whilst sailing upwards with favourable wind, Cartier must soon have become convinced that he was in no Magellan's Strait. The shores approached nearer to one another, the water became brackish, and then sweet, and the current continued against him. Instead of an ocean into which he had hoped to penetrate, he found a beautiful, well-watered, and thickly peopled country.

His first voyage up the river, like all the first steps of Europeans in the new world, may be compared to a triumphal march; for instance, to that of Bacchus to India. To this god, too, he dedicated the first large and beautiful island, filled with fruit-trees and vines, that he met with, calling it "*Ile de Bacchus.*" It was situated in face of the future capital of Quebec.

The astonishment of the wild natives at the advent of the Europeans, their natural curiosity, the joy they experienced at receiving presents of knives, glass beads, metal looking-glasses, and gay ribbons, appears everywhere to have made the first meeting of the two races agreeable. Suspicion and enmity always came later.

Cartier was everywhere received with open arms by the natives, and he gave them banquets on board his ships. Men and women sang and danced, and at all points of the great stream the caziques concluded friendly alliances with him. They brought, too, their sick, their blind, their lame, their mutilated, and weak old men to the river to be cured by him. Cartier pronounced a Pater-noster over them, and hung little copper crosses round their necks, which they were told to kiss. Here and there, too, he erected crosses on the promontories overhanging the river, to consecrate the land to Christianity. And on these crosses he wrote the words: "Over this land rules Francis I., King of France;" words which the wild inhabitants stared at as something mysterious, but which would have caused a great change in their conduct had they understood their meaning.

Occasionally, Cartier thought it advisable to awaken the drowsy echo of the Canadian woods, and to make the trees crash with shots from his cannon. This so astonished the wild natives, that they behaved as if the sky was falling upon their heads, and they howled so terribly, that it seemed to Cartier as if hell was let loose. It amused them more when he now and then ordered his trumpets to be sounded. The banks of the river were charming, often what we should call romantic; for the most part lofty ledges of pointed rocks, or slopes extending to the water's edge, with wood and meadows intermixed. Here and there fruitful plains came in view, covered with Indian corn; for this grain was already cultivated by the natives in that northern land. In the woods on the heights, and on the groups of islands in the river, a great variety of trees flourished, of which oaks, elms, poplars, birch and walnut trees, and especially large spruce and other firs, were the principal. Amidst the dark masses of the latter, the light-green leaves of the sugar sycamores shone out, like oases; and between all these variegated scenes flowed the river, always majestic, broad and interminable, like the deep and constant tones of the base, mingling with the softer and melodious sounds of other instruments in a symphony.

The settlements of the Indians were everywhere numerous, and whenever Cartier pointed to any of them, inquiring the name, he always heard the word Canada in reply. Probably this was nothing more than a general term for village or town. But as the word was constantly repeated, Cartier thought it was meant to apply to the country; the French consequently soon called the whole country Canada, and the stream "*la Grande Rivière de Canada.*"

Having stationed two of his ships in a harbour, not far from the spot where Quebec is now situated, he went up the river in the third, taking with him his boats, and several enterpising young French noblemen. He got as far as an Indian village called Hochelaga, where he came to a bar of rocks, and a rapid, and found that navigation was at an end.

LAND AND WATERS. 71

Canada, and indeed the whole northern half of North America, the entire surface of all the wide districts grouped round Hudson's Bay, consists of broad plateaus or table-lands of granite, which stretch out in succession, or are shoved one upon another, something like large plates of ice when a frozen river is broken up by thaw. On the flat surfaces of these plateaus, extensive rivers flow, or there are large and small lakes, and when the ends of the plateaus are reached, the waters shoot down to other deeper-lying table-lands. According to the height and abruptness of these terraces, the falls are either mere rapids, or waterfalls, called by the French "*saults*" (jumps), or they are powerful cascades, or cataracts. In this way it comes that no other great country in the world is so full of foaming and whirling waters, and again, adjoining these, of smoothly flowing rivers, of stagnant lakes and swamps, alternating with one another for thousands of miles. To one of those waterfalls belongs the Niagara, the king of cataracts.

As the rocky plateaus of this country are often pushed, as it were, as far as the sea, it follows that, occasionally, there are large rivers which, though they flow smoothly in the interior of the land, nevertheless, when they reach the sea, suddenly leap wildly into the briny waves, instead of, as is usually the case, celebrating their nuptials with the ocean in a calm and temperate fashion. Thus it comes that from the decks of ships scenes may be admired which in other lands can only be found by travelling to the high mountains in their interior. As these plateaus sometimes are very far-stretching, there is time for the rivers to grow to great dimensions, and when these breaks in the table-lands occur, the most powerful rivers are seized with a frenzy such as is now unknown to older rivers in other countries.

The cataract region of the great river of Canada begins at once where navigation with sea-ships ceases—at that village of Hochelaga, which, as I have already said, Cartier reached. Here the river, which hitherto had been deep and smooth as a looking-glass, all at once is seen in violent motion. It is split up into a number of seething veins of water, which for many miles wildly toss about, and in masses of white foam wind their way through a labyrinth of dark-coloured rocks. In the midst of this uproar, the Ottawa, the largest tributary of the St. Lawrence, joins its waters to the latter, and in both rivers there is now a continuation of rapids, whirlpools, waterfalls, and cataracts extending upwards for many hundred English miles. From this point there is no other water transport possible, except in the peculiar canoes of the country, made of the bark of birch-trees, which, owing to their elasticity, float amidst the rocks as safely as a fish, whilst their lightness renders them easy to be carried where cataracts occur.

In the harbour of Montreal, which was subsequently built at this spot, long could the singular spectacle be seen, that goods brought in these little canoes were shipped immediately on board sea-going vessels; whilst on our German rivers from the hollow trunks of trees used as boats by our mountaineers, down to the three-masters in our seaports, there is a long catalogue of other intermediate vessels used for the transport of goods.

As Cartier's voyage came to an end at the above-mentioned point, and as he wished at least to have a further view of the country, he ascended a beautifully-shaped hill, which raises its head in this remarkable locality at the union of the waters, and surrounded by arms of the rivers and fertile meadows. From the top of this hill the silver thread of the Ottawa and the rapids of St. Lawrence may be seen shining far away from amidst the dark forests. The inhabitants of Hochelaga told Cartier that at a distance of ten days' journey there was a great sea, out of which the river flowed.

The beautiful hill with the rich and varied view was called by Cartier "*Mont Royal*," and from this circumstance the town, which subsequently was erected at its foot, obtained the name of Mont Real. Cartier now returned to his other ships stationed lower down the river, and as the year was near its close, he wintered there. In the following year he sailed back to France with a whole budget of good and promising news.

It would have been quite enough if Cartier had told his king, Francis, nothing but the simple truth. A vast, navigable, hitherto unknown river, offering the richest fishery in the world, and with fruitful fields on either side; added to this, interminable primeval forests, from which more timber could be cut than the French navy would ever require; in the woods an abundance of wild animals, opening the prospect of a new trade in valuable furs: all these would have formed a sufficiently handsome present for a great monarch. But with such prosaic matters as these neither the heated imaginations of discoverers nor kings could be satisfied. In addition to what he had seen himself with his own eyes, Cartier had gathered a great deal more from his Indians—from their signs and pantomime, for, to be sure, he did not understand their language—and all this information had reference to gold and silver mines and other treasures; so that at last the country really looked just as a discovery in the new world naturally ought to look.

To comprehend the conduct, the expectations, and illusions of Cartier, we must not forget that he himself had but very obscure ideas of the position his Canada occupied on the globe. He, like Columbus, believed he had been in Asia, and with each step that he advanced towards the south-west he expected to reach China or Japan; and the great sea of which the Indians informed him, and which was nothing more than our great Canadian lakes, he held to be a gulf in the South Sea.

Even Francis I. announced to the world in a royal edict that his captain Cartier had made great discoveries in Asia. At that time the idea had not been given up that the upper part of Asia, far to the north of Peru and Mexico, stretched out towards Europe. All the real and imaginary riches connected with the name of Asia were likewise expected to be found in Canada.

Cartier and his contemporaries, starting from this preconceived idea, proceeded therefore when they examined the natives about their country, much as the holy office of the Inquisition had used to do when examining a poor wretch accused of disbelief and heresy, and determined in every case to make out these crimes.

If Cartier showed the Indians the silver whistle of his steersman, or the golden chain presented to him by the king, and asked them if they had ever seen such metals in their country,—if upon this they said they had seen things as shining, it was clear that the land was full of gold and silver mines. But if they shook their heads on being shown such articles, that was not taken as a proof that no mines existed, but merely held to show that the wicked or jealous Indians wished to keep these treasures secret.

From the summit of the Royal Mountain, where the

Indians told him of the great sweet-water sea in the west, Cartier understood them to say that in that direction was the road to a land rich in cinnamon and spices. The Canadians, so he reports, called cinnamon in their language, "*canadeta.*" In the ravine of a rocky part of the great river, the French discovered quarry crystals, and they took them for diamonds. To the present day these rocks, now covered by the works of the citadel of Quebec, are called, "*le Cap des Diamants.*" At other places they found red and green crystals. But they were rubies, emeralds, and turquoises in the eyes of the Frenchmen, and one of the party naïvely remarked at the time: "*Je ne veux pas prétendre qu'ils sont très fins, mais cela fait pourtant plaisir à voir.*"

On discovering the river Saguenay, Cartier pictured to himself a perfect El Dorado at its source. This river, which to this day bears the same name, and which runs into the St. Lawrence to the north of Quebec, is certainly a puzzle; but only to geologists. Its waters fill a very remarkable cleft in the earth, and its depth is unfathomable, being greater than that of the St. Lawrence, and even of the sea near Newfoundland. Cartier, who carefully sounded it at different points, ascertained this fact, and he fancied that such an extraordinary river must lead to most extraordinary things.

On questioning his Indians, he fancied he made out

that the source of this river was in the "kingdom of Saguenay," which abounded in gold, silver, precious stones, and every other valuable product of nature: and this kingdom we see, in fact, like a northern Peru, put down in all the maps of the world made according to Cartier's description. Later pilgrimages in that direction have at least done something to increase our knowledge of the geography of the north.

That to these notions of the country around the source of the Saguenay soon were added wonderful stories of pigmies, giants, and of peoples with one leg, or without heads, was a matter of course. For such like fabulous people, existing only in the imaginations of the men of that period—filled with the fables of Herodotus and other authors of antiquity—were the usual additions to reports of any new discovery of land, from the Straits of Magellan northwards as far as Greenland.

No wonder that, with such accounts in his hands, Francis I. should begin to think of accomplishing great things. He behaved, however, towards his navigator Cartier as Ferdinand had done to Columbus. He held him to be a man of too little importance to make the most of these great things, and to govern a large kingdom. He therefore named one of his noblemen, the Messire Jean François de la Roche, Seigneur de Roberval, to be Viceroy of "New France;" for this

"*Nouvelle France*" was the name with which all that Verrazano and Cartier had discovered—*i. e.* about the whole of North America—was distinguished. To make his deputy still more important, the king bestowed upon him the following seemingly appropriate titles: viz. Lieutenant-General of the Provinces and Kingdoms of Canada, Saguenay, Hochelaga, Terre-Neuve, Baccallaos, or the Cod-fish Land, and Royal General-Intendant of the "Great Fish Banks." He likewise equipped for him a fleet, on board of which numbers of barons, viscounts, and other noblemen entered as volunteers. Cartier, the originator of the whole affair, had to be content to take part in the expedition as chief pilot.

I pass over here the undertakings of this great gentleman, which added little to the work of discovery. Cartier went up his great river once more with this expedition as far as his Mont Royal, and from thence he once more cast his longing gaze towards the unexplored west—his China. But he did not get beyond his former *ne plus ultrà*. Roberval and his noblemen experienced many hardships in that wild land. At length he disappeared entirely in the north, like the Portuguese knight, Cortereal, and so many other northern voyagers, in a manner enveloped in historic darkness. Probably he was wrecked on the coast of Labrador, and lost with all his sailors and ships. With this the glittering bubble burst. In the mean time King Francis died, and Cartier, too, the French Columbus, died in the middle of the same century, in the neighbourhood of his native town, St. Malo, where he had quietly settled down.

No expeditions to North America took place under the kings Henry II., Francis II., and Henry III. This was principally owing to the unquiet state of France during these reigns, and partly because the disappearance of the Viceroy Roberval and his crews had caused great alarm. During the whole of the second half of the sixteenth century the *Nouvelle France* was scarcely anything more than a name. The enterprises of Cartier and Roberval fell at last, in France, so completely into forgetfulness, that not even all the highly remarkable original reports of these voyagers were preserved, and in the end traces of Cartier were sought for, and later discoverers were able to give out their doings for something new.

In our times, to be sure, Cartier, like Columbus, has come into such favour again, that in Canada his Saguenays and Hochelagas are grown quite popular, and— to give here only one instance—travellers may now even put up at inns in that country named after the wild Indian caziques with whom Cartier once had intercourse.

Multa renascentur, quæ jam cecidere, cadentque. In

the history of all human affairs we may observe a certain remarkable ebb and flood. In the discovery of America, too, great progress has been made at certain periods only, some of which are centuries removed from one another. Such especial periods of progress may be found in the history of almost all parts of the new world. In their first attempts the discoverers have often obtained results which afterwards cost very great exertions to regain. Fifty years after Magellan, his strait was so far forgotten that many doubted of its existence. A Spanish poet spoke of the expedition of Magellan as of an *on dit*, and expressed the opinion that, as the strait had never again been heard of, it might have been filled up by an earthquake, or stopped up by blocks of ice.

Soon after the time of Cortez the Mississippi, as I shall have to relate, was well known to the Spaniards; and one hundred and fifty years later the French raked it up again, as it were, out of the total obscurity into which in the mean time it had fallen. The earliest discoveries of the Russians in America, of the English in Baffin's Bay and other districts, fell entirely into forgetfulness, and were not finally made known till the work of discovery had been taken in hand for the second or third time.

This intermittent pulsation, this awakening to fresh

activity after long pauses, may be seen in the development of political events, as a sort of up and down, like the outbreaks and the slumbers of a volcano. The history of the discovery of America yields us this satisfaction, that at least each succeeding effort has been better prepared and more successful than the previous ones; that at least the grandchildren and great-grandchildren have been able to grasp the palm which their ancestors only touched.

The breaks in the progress of the history of Canada are plainly enough connected with the men of genius and of great energy who, from century to century, arose in France under its kings, and who furthered French interests at home and abroad. Francis I., as we have seen, began the work of discovery; the great and good Henry IV. continued it, and Louis le Grand, as will be shown, may be considered as having brought it to a conclusion.

The failures of Roberval and Cartier had produced at least one good result. Whales had been seen by Cartier in great numbers at the mouth of the St. Lawrence. He had brought home, too, some packs of the glossy skins of beavers. Speculators in the ports of Normandy and Brittany turned this knowledge to account, and thus kept up a slight connexion between their country and Canada.

The fishermen and merchants of St. Malo, Cherbourg, Honfleur, La Rochelle, &c., continued their cod-fishing expeditions, and at the same time the whales were pursued to the mouth of the river, the way to which Cartier had pointed out. The men who were employed on these expeditions frequently went up the river, and their usual summer rendezvous was at the mouth of the deep Saguenay, where they boiled their blubber. On this river they were accustomed to meet the Indians, who came down it in their canoes, and if they were not adorned with the diamonds and emeralds of the kingdom of Saguenay, they at least brought with them furs and other produce of their hunting.

The fur-trade now grew into importance. And in consequence of this trade, and especially of beaver-hunting, the French by degrees travelled over and explored the country of the St. Lawrence, and the whole north of America; whilst their successors, the English, from the same cause, at a later period, explored the western portion as far as the Pacific, and the northern as far as the polar seas. Probably about this time the name of St. Lawrence, after the little bay at its mouth which Cartier had dedicated to that saint, came to be applied to the whole river.

A merchant of St. Malo, named Pontgravé, was, properly speaking, the chief promoter and originator of the fur-trade. By repeated voyages to the Saguenay, and the trade in train-oil and the skins of beavers, he realized a fortune. When it became known how profitable this trade had been to him, a company was formed in Rouen, in which many enterprising men took part, and amongst the rest an influential Huguenot, M. de Monts, and another highly energetic nobleman, Samuel de Champlain. De Monts became the director of the company, and Henry IV. gave him an exclusive privilege to trade in furs, for all the lands lying between New York of the present day and Labrador. For, at that time, the kings of France considered all this part of America as belonging to them, although the English likewise laid claim to the whole of the southern portion of it.

M. de Monts, who himself headed many expeditions to America, fixed upon this southern part in especial for his schemes of conquest and discovery; but they were entirely frustrated by the English, who, coming from Virginia, soon destroyed his colony.

In Samuel de Champlain, however, the French found a man who led them to great things; for he was possessed of distinguished and statesmanlike qualities, and determination of purpose. It was he who, fixing his eyes specially on the north of New France, the river St. Lawrence, in the course of a long and active life established the power of France in these districts, and may be called the creator and father of Canada.

Above all, Champlain founded a settlement on the St. Lawrence, a thing long desired in France. He chose for this purpose the point indicated by nature, where, near the Bacchus Island, the principal narrowing of the majestic stream, a change from a gulf-like appearance to that of a narrow channel, takes place. To this point the largest sea-going vessels can sail with ease. It had long been named by the Indians Quebejo, also Quelobec, which meant narrowing of the river; and from these words, the name Quebec has been derived.

The sweet-water sea in the west, of which his predecessor, Cartier, had long ago reported, raised likewise in Champlain the old hope to find there a passage to the South Sea and China. He got his Indians to sketch out the outline, and give him a description of the lakes in the west as far as they knew them, and he heard that the hindermost and largest lake was quite salt, and so long that no one had ever seen the end of it. He thought this must be the South Sea, and he hoped that his Quebec, in which, in 1608, he built his first wooden huts, would come to be a town of great importance. He intended to make it the principal depôt for the transit of goods from the South Sea to the Atlantic, to raise it to be something like what San Francisco in California is at the present day.

Champlain and his companions were the first to become acquainted with the Indian tribes, the Hurons, the Algonquins, and the Iroquois—names which were unknown to Cartier, but which have been preserved to the present day. The Hurons and Algonquins lived on the left bank of the great river; the Iroquois on the right bank, to the south. These tribes from the opposite sides of the river had long been at war with one another. Champlain took part with the northern Indians, and he went with them to the south in their expeditions against the Iroquois, who, after this, constantly opposed the French, allying themselves with the Dutch, and at a later period with their successors, the English of New York and Boston.

The Iroquois were accustomed to come from the interior on their plundering excursions down a tributary of the St. Lawrence, called by the French the River Richelieu. Champlain, with his Hurons and three French musketeers, took this way to look for them. This led him to the discovery of a long and smiling lake, out of which the river came, and to this day it is called Lake Champlain.

Like a knight of olden times in search of adventures, and accompanied only by one faithful groom, Champlain made excursions up the Saguenay, and up the Ottawa, and other rivers not explored by Cartier, so that he was the first to fire off a musket in these districts. He has been called the "knight-errant of Canada;" but he wandered about to some purpose. Along with his taste for adventures, which in those days even statesmen shared, the idea of founding a new state interested him most. He had a great capacity for colonisation, and all along the St. Lawrence there is scarcely any old position of importance not connected with Champlain's name.

His trying journeys, his wars, and his negotiations with the Indians, caused him, as had been the case with Columbus, much less suffering and trouble than the political intrigues in his fatherland. After the death of the good King Henry IV., there was a constant change of viceroys for New France. Now the Prince of Condé, now the Marshal de Montmorency, and now a Duke de Ventadour, was placed at the head of the affairs of a country which none of these men had ever seen. One of their doings was to take away the old privileges from a trading company, to give similar privileges to a new one. Champlain was frequently called back to France by affairs of this kind, and, like Columbus, he was obliged, times without end, to give up his exploring journeys and the founding of settlements.

The interest, however, which Cardinal Richelieu and other influential men, following his example, subsequently took in Champlain's undertakings, at length crowned his efforts with success. He was appointed governor of Canada, and died as such in the year 1635, in Quebec, the town which he had called into life. His remains are deposited there, like as the body of Columbus has been placed in Cuba, and that of Cortez in Mexico.

Champlain had not only trading speculations and colonisation at heart, but, like nearly all the earlier discoverers, he took especial interest in the spread of Christianity and the conversion of heathens. He is reported to have said that "the salvation of a soul was of more value than the conquest of a kingdom." Twenty years before his death he invited some Mendicant monks, and ten years later he called the Jesuits to his aid. From the St. Lawrence these brothers soon spread amongst the natives, either by following in the footsteps of Champlain and the French fur-traders, or else preceding and opening a way for the latter.

We are greatly indebted to the Jesuit missionaries for the further disclosure of the districts around the St. Lawrence. They were, for the most part, brave and well-informed men, who, now travelling on foot, now in the bark canoes of the country, extended their excursions far to the north. Almost all the subsequent discoveries of importance were under their direction, and from their careful reports a knowledge of a large portion of North America has been derived. And, in especial, they were the first to explore and make known that wonderful basin, that lake system of the west of Canada, in all its extent and capabilities.

Much has been sung and said about the four or five brilliant stars in the Southern Cross, but these five Canadian lakes which it has pleased nature to develop in the upper regions of the St. Lawrence, spread more light on this earth, and are still more worthy of the poet's praise.

Taken together, they exceed the Caspian Sea in extent. Not one of them but is about the size of a German kingdom. Their basins are deeply hollowed out, and in some places they are twice the depth of the Baltic in its deepest parts. They are therefore as navigable for large vessels as the sea, and this, too, for a distance of between eight and nine hundred miles in the middle of a continent. The waters of all are sweet, and those of the largest lake are so clear and so agreeable to the taste that they are in great request, and transported to distant places.

Each of the more western of these lakes lies upon higher table-land than its neighbour, and the isthmuses which separate them are pierced by canals, in which the waters that pour from the upper lakes form numerous cataracts and whirlpools. Large peninsulas extend into these basins, like vast wedges, separating them from one another. These peninsulas are remarkable for fertility and beauty, and each one forms the main territory of a separate state, viz. of Upper Canada, Michigan, and Wisconsin. The produce of these lake-peninsulas is greater than the kingdom of Saguenay. Two of them abound in the most fruitful corn-fields, and the third has hidden under its woods such a wealth in metals, in iron and copper ore, that here only the *embarras de richesses,* the difficulty of breaking up and transporting such masses, checks their being turned to account.

An obscure report of the existence of these lakes reached, as we have said, the ears of Cartier, and after him we find a "*mare dulcium aquarum*" (a sweet-water sea) figure in all the maps of the new world, the outlines of which, however, were sketched in a very vague manner. Some geographers made it in connexion with the South Sea; others fancied it to be a bay of the Arctic Sea, for which, as is known, the Caspian Sea was once held, until its northern end was discovered. The second great explorer of Canada, Champlain, knew, to be sure, something more about these lakes. He knew that there were several basins, and the one most to the east, Lake Ontario, he had himself reached and made the circuit of. But even he held fast to the idea that these lakes were in connexion with the South Sea, and, as I have already said, he got out of his Indians, by questioning them, that the hindermost of them, in its western portion, again became "salt."

The Jesuit missionaries, who were destined to solve

this problem, entered into these inner lake regions in two ways, both natural channels of communication: one to the south-west, along the main stream, the St. Lawrence; the other to the north-west, along the principal tributary, the oft-named Ottawa. By the first way, which led them into the territories exposed to the inroads of the wild Iroquois, they came upon the Lakes Ontario and Erie.

Many of the bold missionaries who penetrated into these wilds met with the death of martyrs. But others were always ready to come forward and follow in the footsteps of their predecessors. They attempted, in especial, but long in vain, to check the savage fury of the Iroquois, who, from the south, threatened the milder tribe of the Hurons, and the French colonists themselves, with destruction. In the year 1640, the first missionary, Father Brébœuf, came in this direction as far as the falls of Niagara, of which he gave a glowing description. Others following him, built their little forest chapels— which the savages sometimes burnt down — on the southern shores of those lakes; set up missionary stations—which were often destroyed—and began the work again where their predecessors, killed by the Iroquois, had left it. Thus, by degrees, they worked their way round both the lakes, Ontario and Erie, which, however, at the time, went by the names of "Cats' Lake" and "Lake Frontenac."

The other way, along the Ottawa, was somewhat less thorny than the south-western pilgrimage to the terrible Iroquois. For, in the first direction, dwelt the somewhat milder races of the Hurons and Algonquins, who sometimes were glad to have a missionary amongst them, and occasionally even begged the great "Ononthion" (for so they called the French Governor-General of Canada, and also the King of France) to give them one. When they acted thus, however, it was not so much from any pious longing for Christianity, as the Jesuits fancied, as from the superstition that the prayers of the missionaries had power over the wild animals they hunted. Besides, they looked upon the missionaries as a means of enticing the fur-traders and other colonists, who usually followed in their track, and with whom they liked to have dealings.

A missionary, when "Ononthion" had granted their request, was often as favourably situated with the Indians as their way of life would allow. They took him with them in their canoes, and if he showed himself capable of supporting the toils and privations of Indian forest excursions, if his prayers proved useful to banish bad weather and to charm the fish and wild animals, they made much of him, and brought their children to be baptised. But, on the other hand, if things did not go favourably, they would treat their spiritual chief and teacher as their servant and slave. And if he did not render them good service, they became thoroughly tired of him, took from him his useless prayer-books, and threw them into the water, driving him from them into the forests; or they even killed him when at his prayers, as a troublesome and superfluous member of their community.

In the year 1660 the Jesuit Mesnard accepted an invitation of this kind, and, with a troop of friendly Indians, he worked his way up the then not unbeaten path of the Ottawa. He took his turn at rowing with the Indians, helped them to carry their boats when they came to cataracts, swam like one of themselves; and if there was want of food, he fished, or pounded the bones of the wild animals which he collected, and boiled them up into broth. In this manner he reached the upper district of the Ottawa, and from thence he went over with his Indians to the northern shore of Lake Huron. He found there the celebrated cataracts, which he dedicated to the Virgin Mary, and which to this day are called the "St. Mary Falls;" and he likewise reached the great "*Lac Supérieur*," the largest and most remote of Canadian lakes, which he was the first to discover.

He passed the winter on the southern shore of this lake, giving the names of various saints to its capes and bays. In the following spring, Father Mesnard, always trusting in Him who feeds the birds of the air, and having at times no other nourishment than such as could be obtained from the pounded bark of trees and moss, penetrated into the western portion of the lake, to look, as he said, even in this hiding-place, for souls for Christ. To the groups of small islands which he found in that direction he gave the name of the "Apostles' Islands," which they are called to this day.

But he never came out of this corner again. Having quitted his companions, he disappeared in a wood, and it has never been ascertained how he lost his life. Many years afterwards his breviary, his waistband, and a portion of his journal were discovered in the tent of a Sioux Indian on the Upper Mississippi; and it was remarked that these savages held the relics of this martyr in great veneration, making them offerings of food and other things at their meals, as they did to their spirits.

Not long after it had become known at Quebec—where news of him had been anxiously expected—that this messenger to the far west had been lost, the Indians from from the Upper Lake again came with the request for a missionary. This the authorities demurred in granting. But the apostolic men, it is said, opposed the opinion of their superiors, and this time Father Allouez, a man still more celebrated in the history of the discovery of Canada than Mesnard, joined the four hundred Indians who had come for him, and went with them to the northwest.

In the year 1666 Father Allouez reached the cataracts of St. Mary and the Upper Lake. At first, like his predecessor, he travelled along the southern shore about one hundred leagues, lived two years near the Apostles' Islands, where Mesnard had disappeared, and built himself there a small chapel. His reputation spread in the neighbourhood; from far and near the Indians brought him their children and sick, and came to look at his religious services and listen to his prayers in a spirit of reverence. The good missionary held communication with more than twelve nations. By means of the far-spread language of the Algonquins, which in these regions plays about the same part as French in Europe, he was able to make himself understood by these people. We now hear for the first time the names of many Indian nations, which are still known, and in part have become celebrated as the names of states of the American confederation. For instance, the name of "Illinois," now applied to a great river and large state, and that of "Knistinaux," are far spread in the north at the present day.

From all these people Father Allouez derived information about the nature of the countries they came from. The most remarkable was the news he gathered from the Sioux, who came from a great distance. Their country, they said, extended to the north to the end of the habitable world. To the west there were other nations, in the rear of whom, however, the land was cut off, and there was the "great stinking water." They described to him the beautiful wide prairies of their own country, on which numerous herds of cows browsed, and the great river where many beavers dwelt, and which was called "Messepi." In the far west was the home of a terrible kind of bears of enormous size and strength, and many of their people fell a sacrifice to them. This is, without doubt, the now so celebrated, and in the west so much dreaded, "grizzly bear," with which American travellers at a later period became acquainted in the Rocky Mountains, and of which, as of many other animals, the first information was obtained through Father Allouez.

From his little mission and chapel Father Allouez made many excursions in the neighbourhood. He travelled, too, along the northern shore of the lake, and reached at last its extreme western end, which terminates in a pointed bay, like the form of a wedge. This point has since been called "*Fond du Lac.*" A river runs into it, which Father Allouez, in honour of the king then reigning in France, called the River St. Louis.

This little River St. Louis is the most western water

of the whole St. Lawrence region, and as it is at the same time the largest contributor to the Upper Lake, it may be looked upon as the source of that powerful river. "New France," so often a prey to storms, was in the enjoyment at that time of a profound and beneficial peace, of which advantage was taken in the cause of discovery and extension of power. New missionaries came over from France to America, and hastened after Father Allouez; the Father Claude Dablon, the Father Marquette (the celebrated discoverer of the Mississippi), and many others. The two just named were posted to the mission at the "Falls of St. Mary." Others were sent to other branches of the Algonquins, who came up in numbers, since just at that time the Iroquois left them at peace. It was now that the south-west branch of the great Canadian lake system was first discovered. This lake, Michigan, or, as it was first called, "Lake Illinois," had continued unknown the longest.

Here, too, Father Allouez took the lead. He travelled, or, as the Jesuits called it, "worked," in a beautiful vineyard, in that fair land to the west of the just-named lake, where green meadows and woods of beautiful foliage, in which vines, wild plum, apple, and walnut trees abound. The humid lower grounds nearest the rivers were covered with wild corn (called by the French, *folle avoine*), which served the Indians for food, and on which, too, the large "woolly Illinois oxen" (for so Father Allouez calls the buffaloes) likewise fed. It was a part of the fertile and now so much valued territory of Wisconsin.

The long journeys of Father Allouez, together with those of Father Marquette, may be considered to have concluded the discovery of the St. Lawrence, and completed the knowledge of Canada, at least in its main features. In the year 1672 the Jesuits were able to present to the great King Louis a map they had made, on which were drawn tolerably correctly the outlines of all the Canadian lakes, and their connexion with the St. Lawrence.

Like as in the history of great wars, so in the history of discovery, the muse has only put down the great names of those individuals who have performed something decisive, who have worked with intelligence and consciousness, and given a marked progress to our knowledge. But just as the main bodies of armies have their light corps of sharpshooters, skirmishers, and volunteers, who are the first to enter the enemy's land, to bring down their opponents, and the first to make roads and bridges, so there was in Canada, in addition to the privileged government officials, to the Pope's consecrated messengers, an obscure mass of private persons, who, on their own account, sought adventures in the wilderness;

often accompanying those missionaries and officials, but often, too, preceding them, and showing them the way, or else following in the tracks of the prominent heroes, and then adding to the details of geographical knowledge.

The class of men called in Canada "*coureurs des bois*" (wood-runners), became conspicuous soon after the kings of France had bestowed privileges upon their merchants and officers, and it increased in numbers and importance the more the discoveries and the fur-trade in Canada extended, and the more these monopolies were found to interfere with the interests of the public in general.

Enterprising individuals, dissatisfied with these restraints on commerce, followed the example of Champlain, shouldered their muskets, and pushed up one of the rivers not yet occupied by the privileged, or the servants of the Church; or they arrived at lakes not yet explored, gained an influence with Indian tribes not yet baptised, purchasing from them their beaver-skins on their own account. Frequently these men accommodated themselves to the mode of life of the Indians, whom they accompanied, as welcome allies, on their hunting or war excursions.

Not only did they follow the example of Champlain, but of the Jesuit missionaries too. Like them they prayed over the sick, or made the sign of the cross over the dying, performed wonders, and told the wild Indians bible histories, which pleased those children of nature so exceedingly, that they often repaid them with whole packs of beaver-skins. Simply as story-tellers, these "*coureurs des bois*" have often attained great influence and wealth amongst the Indians, for whom they wrote down on bits of paper the names of Mary, Joseph, Moses, and the prophets, demanding to be paid for such amulets with the skins of beavers.

These remarkable wood-runners, men with hardened frames, and well acquainted with the nature of the country and the customs of the natives, have in the end completed the work of the Cartiers, Champlains, and the Jesuits. They ventured wherever a beaver or a bear could live; and from the Canadian lakes they have spread themselves over the whole of the wide north-west of America. They have given the names now in use to almost all the localities. They have circulated amongst the people in Canada the report of every new lake, river, or range of mountains; and they reached the Rocky Mountains, and lastly—associated in the first instance with the British, and later with the North Americans—the South Sea.

The British and the United States beaver-hunters were their pupils, and it was only by the aid of the French Canadians that they found their way in the western labyrinth. Even our modern Franklins have required the assistance of these men to reach the polar seas ; and, next to the English, there is no other language so spread throughout North America, as the French.

Amongst the so-called wood-runners, beaver and fur hunters of Canada, occasionally there were very clever men, some of whom belonged to the educated classes. Through them many admirable descriptions of countries when first discovered, and many accounts of primitive modes of life, have been added to our literature.

If we now take a survey of the history of the discovery of Canada in its totality, the following is the result. We see that fish, especially whales and cod-fish, were the first to show the French the way to the gates of the country; that in the reign of Francis I. fabulous stories and hopes of El Doradoes led them through these gates; that under Henri IV. the rumour of the sweet-water sea, and the hope built upon it of reaching the South Sea and China, led them into the interior; that under Louis XIV. zeal in gaining converts brought them to the end of the Great River, and that the animals with valuable furs at length did the rest.

The French, however, who for the most part only filled Canada with monks and adventurers, got scarcely beyond this fur-hunting—which is but the rudest way of turning a country to account—and beyond that hunting for souls, which, with all the zeal bestowed upon it, has produced but few lasting results.

It is only since they lost the country to the British, *i.e.* since 1761, that it has been gained in the full sense for Europe and humanity. Only since then have all its capabilities been discovered, and those inner treasures disclosed which had continued hidden to the French. Since that time has begun a much more profitable kind of hunting, that after fertile fields and useful metals, after convenient harbours and localities in which to build new towns. The French of Louis XV.'s time consoled themselves for the loss of the country about which their Cartiers, Champlains, and their great monarchs had displayed such enthusiasm and energy, by saying, "What have we in fact sacrificed in Canada but a few snow-fields more or less."

But these "snow-fields" have given the lie in a striking manner to those witty courtiers of a weak king. They now yield an income of more than 30,000,000*l.*, and have a population of more than five million Christians. The block-house stations of the fur-hunters have been transformed into large emporiums of commerce; the Indian villages, in which a Jesuit had once set up a little wooden chapel, have grown into a wreath of splendid towns, reflected in the clear lakes; and on these lakes, where formerly a praying missionary or an adventurous *coureur des bois* glided along in a bark canoe, now may be seen whole fleets of floating wooden palaces, flying backwards and forwards like weavers' shuttles, and adding to the webb of the world's commerce.

In all the corners of the Upper Lake, in each of its bays and harbours, has this commerce taken root, and sown the seeds from which new towns, like fresh blossoms, will come forth. Neither the old *Kabeljau* fishers of Honfleur, nor Cartier of St. Malo, with his imagination full of the gold mines and one-legged people of the kingdom of Saguenay, nor Samuel Champlain with his longing for China, ever dreamt that their undertakings were the preludes to such brilliant results.

CHAPTER III.

THE MISSISSIPPI AND THE JESUITS.

The Captains of Governor Garay discover the Mouths of the Mississippi (1519)—Pamphilo de Navaez is lost at the Mouths of the Mississippi (1529)—Cabeza de Vaca wanders about for nine Years in the Lands to the south-west of the Mississippi (1529-1537)—Fernando de Soto discovers and navigates the Lower Mississippi (1540-1542)—Moscoso's Retreat (1543) — The Jesuit Marquette goes down the entire Mississippi in a Canoe (1673).

OF all the noble rivers which, like arteries, extend over the continent of America, the Mississippi certainly deserves the palm. Its size and the position it occupies in a political and culture-historical respect, cause it to be the most important of all.

It has the advantage of all great rivers whose course is from north to south, that it passes through many zones, and connects regions of varied produce with one another. Whilst the St. Lawrence, flowing from west to east, passes through cold countries only; whilst the Amazon and the Orinoco, both running parallel to the equator, flow only through regions of tropical heat; the Mississippi springs out of the pine forests of the north, and sweeps down to the hot sugar-fields of the Gulf of Mexico. The La Plata is the only other American river resembling it somewhat in this respect, and it might be called the Mississippi of the south.

In its course through the heart of North America, at almost equal distance from the Atlantic and Pacific oceans, the Mississippi receives on the one side all the waters of the Alleghanies, and on the other all those of the Rocky Mountains, spreading out between them a wonderful system of navigable canals connected through the great central stream. It stands there, like a gigantic production of nature, with its far-reaching arms, adapted to bring into connexion the most fruitful states of North America. It may be compared to an Atlas bearing on his shoulders the western and eastern portions of this division of the globe.

The numerous tumuli and other remarkable earthworks and monuments, which in modern times have been discovered and examined on the banks of the Mississippi, have proved that this river has likewise a history of great antiquity. It appears that half-civilised nations have formerly been spread far up its valleys, but that here, too, as elsewhere, destructive migrations and extensive convulsions have taken place, and that an age of iron has alternated with an age of gold. But the history of these events reaches so far back, that it is as dark and turbid as the waters of the Missouri.

Happily, we have not to occupy ourselves here with attempts to throw light upon this subject. We have only to relate by what circumstances this gigantic watercourse and its labyrinth of valleys were first made known to Europeans.

The renown of having been the first to introduce some knowledge of America's greatest river belongs to a contemporary and rival of Cortez, the Spanish governor of Jamaica, Francisco de Garay, who sent a fleet to the unknown shores in the north, where he hoped to find a second Mexico. His captains discovered and sailed along for the first time the whole of the flat, sandy, and uninviting north coast of the bay into which flow the waters of the Mississippi (the Gulf of Mexico), and they brought home the unwelcome news that a desolate land from Florida to the mountains of Mexico bent round in the form of a bow. In the middle of this bow, however, they said that a great river poured out its waters, which they had named the river of the Holy Ghost ("*Rio del Espiritu Santo*").

It is in the highest degree improbable that these captains of Governor Garay executed the difficult experiment of sailing into the mouth of the barricaded Mississippi. But its dirty waters whirl far enough out upon the heavy salt waves to be perceptible at a great distance. Besides, the trunks of trees, large floating masses of wood, bushes, and other refuse of the forests, which the stream sweeps down into the sea, make known its existence at a distance of fifty English miles from the shore. For some time the Spaniards continued to call the Mississippi—which they may be said rather to have received intimation of, than to have discovered—the Holy River; and the large unexplored country in the north was named on the oldest Spanish maps, the Land of Garay. ("*Tierra de Garay*").

About eight years after the above expedition, Garay having died in the mean time, the governor, Pampilo de Navaez, another celebrated contemporary and rival of Cortez, decided on trying his luck " in the north." He thought that behind the uninviting shore a beautiful and rich interior might be hidden. To explore this interior, he landed with a small army, equipped at his own expense, on the coast of Florida, and he then began to march about both to the north and the west, along the Gulf of Mexico. But this march came to a disastrous end.

The wild and impassable character of the country, and the bold and hostile races in Florida, placed great difficulties in his way. His troops, decimated by hunger and the arrows of the Indians, soon were in a wretched state. After a year of toilsome marching about and fruitless exertions, he at length decided to return across the sea, and in place of ships he constructed boats as well as could be managed. But these fragile vessels were caught in a storm near the dangerous mouth of the Mississippi, and Navaez with all his remaining followers but one were swallowed by the waves.

The man who escaped from this wreck was one of Navaez's officers, called Cabeza de Vaca (the Cow's-head), who became celebrated for his extensive travels and extraordinary adventures. He contrived to gain the good-will of the savage races in the north of the Gulf of Mexico by making himself in various ways useful to them. He was inventive, and he served them now as their slave, now as an industrious trader, now as their doctor and adviser, so that he was looked upon as a wonderful being, and was able not only to preserve his life amongst these savages, but to pass freely from tribe to tribe, often as a chief and clever leader in their wars. In this way, in the course of nine years, he wandered over the prairies of Texas of the present day, and across the mountains to the north of Mexico, where he appeared suddenly amongst his countrymen, who too regarded him with astonishment and wonder.

The extraordinary things that this Cabeza de Vaca afterwards related to the Emperor Charles V., his reports of lovely valleys, of grand rivers and mountains abounding in metals, of the land of cow-herds (as he called the prairies of Texas with their herds of buffaloes), again excited the imaginations of the Spaniards, who, since the destruction of Governor Navaez, had thought no more about the lands to the north of the Gulf of Mexico.

And now the remarkable man entered upon the scene who passes for the first Spanish discoverer of the Mississippi, and who, as such, is represented in all his glory on a large and celebrated wall-painting in the Capitol of Washington. We must therefore say a few words about his wonderful doings and extraordinary fate.

Fernando de Soto, for this was his name, is reckoned by the Spaniards to be one of the four first and most distinguished "*conquistadores*" of the new world, the other three being Columbus, Cortez, and Pizarro.

Like these, Soto was the son of a poor Spanish nobleman, who, as an historian expresses it, possessed nothing but his coat of arms, his sword, and his shield. As a young man eager for action he went to the West Indies, and with Pizarro to Peru. He was that often-mentioned knight whose portrait figures in many pictures; who, as envoy of Pizarro, was the first to see the Inca Atabalipa, and whose foaming and rearing steed struck the suite of the Inca with astonishment and terror.

Soto was likewise one of the three emissaries whom Pizarro, directly after his first successes, sent to the golden Cuzco, and who were the first Europeans to make this long journey through the valleys of the Andes. Subsequently, he received a splendid portion of the spoils of Peru, the division of the Inca's treasure alone bringing him in 100,000 ducats for his share. Having thus obtained wealth and greatness, he, like many others, grown tired of Pizarro's rule, left him and returned to Spain. This must have been about the year 1536.

He made his appearance with great splendour. He was liberal and generous, and the reputation of being a bold and enterprising leader had preceded him. He was in the prime of life, and an author who was acquainted with him, describes his person as stately and well made, his countenance cheerful and kindly, somewhat dark in colour (*moreno de color*), and his " bearing equally good on horseback or on foot." He was, therefore, soon surrounded by a number of friends and protégés, and he found no difficulty in obtaining the hand of the noble and beautiful Doña Isabella de Bobadilla, a lady belonging to one of the most illustrious houses of Spain.

But the intoxication which seized him, like all the others who had taken part in plundering the new world, the ungovernable thirst for gold, desire of territory, and craving for adventures, did not allow him to remain long quiet. Like all these pupils of Cortez, these swordgirded apostles of Pizarro, he fancied that there must be other Incas, Perus, and Montezumas to be found. And as he saw all the new countries in South America already occupied, he turned his eyes to the north, where no attempts had been made since the terrible loss of Governor Navaez, and where, as it seemed, he could rule undisturbed.

He therefore petitioned the emperor for the right of discovery and conquest in Florida; for this name, which the Spaniards had originally given only to a peninsula, had gradually been extended—as already pointed out— to the whole of the broad territories to the north of Cuba. Under this word was comprised, not only the present United States, but also Canada. Charles V. granted his request, and gave him in addition the governorship of the Island of Cuba, as a necessary base of operations, as a safe point of departure and retreat, as a magazine for stores, and harbour for equipment.

Excited by the grandeur of the campaign and the renown of the leader, men thirsting for action poured in from all sides. Amongst them were many noblemen, and even knights, from the neighbour-country of Portugal. Things wore the appearance of preparations for a crusade. Many young heirs sold their birthrights, invested the capital thus obtained in the enterprise, and girded on the sword with which they hoped to achieve greatness. Some of the most distinguished courtiers of the emperor were unable to resist the entreaties of their sons, and gave the intoxicated youths permission to take part in the expedition. Many of these noblemen were accompanied by their young wives, and Soto likewise took with him his fair Doña Isabella. With this, too, as with all the other crusades to the new world, there was no lack of priests and monks for the conversion of the heathens in North America.

Soto was unable to accept all the offers he received, so he formed a corps of about one thousand picked men in the prime of life. With these, in ten ships of war and twenty merchant vessels, he sailed from the Guadalquiver in the spring of 1535. This great armament went forth upon the path of death, for very few of those who took part in it were destined ever to see their fatherland again.

In Cuba, which was then full of herds of cattle that had become wild, the expedition was furnished with fresh provisions. Above all things many pigs, always the companions of the Spaniards on their distant expeditions, were taken on board. Soto paid particular attention to have his troops well mounted. He knew by experience how greatly horses terrified the natives of America; and at that time Cuba was the country which supplied Mexico and neighbouring lands with those noble animals. For himself, he selected a body-guard of sixty lances.

When he had settled the affairs of his government in Cuba, appointed new officials, and installed his wife as regent in his absence, he sailed for Florida. Several rich planters in Cuba, veterans from the time of Velasquez, joined his expedition, some of them with their vassals, and servants, and negro slaves.

Soto and his followers, like their unfortunate predecessor Navaez, landed on the west side of the narrow peninsula of Florida of the present day, which they greeted as the land of promise, and then, like Navaez, they marched into the interior.

His earliest exploits, though remarkable in themselves, are of no importance for our history. In the first instance, fighting continually with the natives, he advanced in a north-easterly direction through the present states of Georgia and Carolina. But as he here did not meet with the northern Atabalipa he was looking for, he gradually turned to the west. This march took up a whole year, and his army grew like an avalanche. For not only did the herds of cattle he had brought with him increase on the verdant pastures of Florida, but the prisoners of war were added to his army as slaves, every

Spaniard receiving some for his service. This avalanche was destined, however, soon to melt away like an icicle exposed to the sun.

Soto soon gained the experience that in Florida the children of the soil differed as completely from the enervated and oppressed subjects of the Incas and Montezumas, as that land itself did from Peru. Although his army was much greater than those of Cortez or Pizarro, and neither he himself was wanting in military talent nor his followers in courage, still he was not able to accomplish such heroic and brilliant deeds as those great leaders had done.

All the combats with the independent skin-clad tribes of hunters in North America were on both sides very sanguinary, and the horses did not produce the same effects in inspiring terror as in Peru. In one of the battles these noble animals were killed by dozens; and at the conclusion of another combat six hundred Spaniards had seven hundred wounds to bind up. But the hardest blow Soto and his companions received was in their winter quarters in the "land of the Chickasaws," not far from the Mississippi. They had built for themselves a town of huts, made of straw and reeds, and surrounded it with a wall and ditch. This encampment was suddenly attacked by the wild Indians, led by one of their caziques, a "*malignant traitor*," as the

Spaniards call him, but without doubt a *brave patriot* in the eyes of the natives.

After surprising the sentries in the dead of the night, the Indians in great numbers stormed the encampment, and with horrible war yells, and bearing lighted torches in their hands, they set the town of straw on fire. Many Christians were put to death in sleep; a large quantity of arms, their store of powder, their horses and cattle, were lost in the flames. Here, amongst the wild natives of Florida, the same fate well-nigh befel Soto that Arminius met with amongst the Germans in the Teutoburger forest. His terrified soldiers dispersed themselves. It was the first time that a large corps of Spaniards fled before Americans. Soto, who always slept in his armour, got his men again together, and at last drove his enemy from the field. But it was difficult to replace the loss of European arms and tools. The Spaniards had to construct forges on the smouldering ruins of their encampment to enable them to make the weapons serviceable that had been injured by the flames. The bellows for these forges were constructed of the skins of buffaloes, and the barrels of old firelocks. New staffs for their lances were cut in the forests. The good European woollen cloaks had to be replaced by mats which they learnt to make of reeds, after the fashion of the natives.

Breeches were made of the skins of deer, and waistcoats and jackets of those of the wild cats. In place of their iron armour the skins of the wild cows supplied covering for their feet, and also shields, and instead of helmets they made themselves caps of the skins of bears.

Clothed in this extraordinary way, more resembling a horde of Tartars than young Spanish noblemen and Castilian heirs, they drew near to the Mississippi. The loss of their European salt was the cause of much misery and disease. They learned, however, from their Indian prisoners that the ashes of a certain herb contained a little salt, and they searched for it everywhere, mixing its ashes with their food. They likewise followed the buffaloes to certain places (the so-called buffalo licks), where the earth is salty, and they extracted as much of this salt as possible.

Rising from their winter quarters like phœnixes—but, as phœnixes, wonderfully changed and robbed of their fine feathers—the Spaniards at length DISCOVERED THE GREAT RIVER, of which they had long heard, THE HIGH BANKS OF THE MISSISSIPPI of our day. The Indians thereabouts called it "Chucagua," and they counted twelve different names of the river in use amongst other tribes. Soto's Spanish biographers usually call it "*el Rio Grande de la Florida*" (the

Great River of Florida). It was the same to which, as we have seen, the contemporaries of Cortez gave the name of the Holy Ghost River.

When Soto and his companions stepped upon the high banks, and beheld the sweeping flood of water, their hopes revived. To such a powerful stream, they thought, must belong a powerful kingdom. They built boats and rafts to proceed up the river, and again began to question the natives about a great Indian monarch. These Indians naturally knew of a cazique somewhere or other, who, to their poor ideas, was a very powerful personage; and thus Soto was led from the "cazique of Chiska" to the "cazique of Chasquina," and from the last to the "cazique of Capaha," and so on to others. But they were none of them Montezumas. They were merely uncivilised, poor, and half-naked princes, ruling over tribes of hunters.

Of these chiefs, who occasionally met Soto in a friendly spirit, he made inquiries about the nature of the northern countries. He also made religious speeches to them about the mysteries of the Christian faith, teaching them to make the sign of the cross, as every Spanish discoverer held it to be his duty to do. Occasionally he made his priests and monks display the ceremonies of the Christian church on the banks of the Mississippi, and get up great processions, which highly pleased the Indians, and attracted them from great distances.

When, at length, he had reached the district to the south of the point where the Ohio joins its waters to those of the Mississippi, and his prospects still did not improve; where, on the contrary, he gathered from the Indians that, to the north, the country became more wild, so that only herds of buffaloes could exist in it, he gave up this direction.

But he planted here, at his northern *non plus ultrà*, an enormous cross, as Godfrey of Bouillon had done on the walls of Jerusalem. For this purpose the Spaniards dragged the largest trees that could be found in the forests to a hill on the banks of the Mississippi, where they put up the cross. All now passed round it, like pilgrims, in solemn procession, for this ceremony was meant, at the same time, as a formal taking possession of the country in the name of the emperor. It is said that twenty-nine thousand Indians had come together on this occasion, and that they held up their hands to Heaven as if in prayer.

Soto now turned to the west. He had heard of mountains in that direction, in which he again hoped to find his El Dorado. In a tedious march, during the year 1541, he passed through the territory of the even now but little populated state of Arkansas. But the Mexican mountains were far, and, disappointed in his hopes, he at last found it necessary to return to the Mississippi, on the banks of which river were cultivated fields of Indian corn, woods abounding in vines, walnut, and other fruit-trees, and where roebucks and other kinds of deer were more frequently met with.

It was no wonder that these unceasing and fruitless marches at length made the troops impatient and dissatisfied, and long to return to Cuba and Spain. But Soto, whose firmness of purpose nothing could turn, had no sooner become aware of this spirit amongst his followers than he stepped upon a large stone in the centre of the camp, and rated both men and officers in terms of greatest severity. He demanded of every man, he said, the performance of his duty, and the obedience due to himself. After their brilliant departure from their country, he expected that they would all feel ashamed, as he should do, to appear again before their young wives and the emperor in such miserable guise, dressed in furs and skins like barbarians. As for himself, he added, he was determined to explore this land further, until he had found the great king of the north. And he wished them to understand that as long as he had the command no one need flatter himself with the hope of leaving Florida until this task should be fulfilled.

This speech, which Soto delivered with proud bearing and threatening tone of voice, had the effect of silencing his followers and confirming them in their obedience; for they all knew that Soto was not the man to be trifled with. Nevertheless, this speech was like the song of the dying swan.

The following spring, when they had again taken up their quarters on the banks of the Mississippi, a profound melancholy came over Soto, for he felt himself thoroughly disappointed in all his expectations. He who until now had been a pattern to all in bearing privations and sufferings, who had always shown himself cheerful and ready, the first in every danger, suddenly broke down. He was seized with violent fever, which carried him off in a few days. Before his death, he took leave in a touching manner of all his companions, and appointed the second in command, Luis de Moscoso, to be his successor. The Spaniards, fearing that if they were to bury their illustrious dead in the usual way, the Indians would disturb his grave, cut down one of the largest trees they could find, hollowed it out, and placed the coffin in its centre, together with many heavy stones. In the dead of night, and shedding many tears, they sank the tree into the bed of the river, like as their distant ancestors, the west Goths, had done with the body of their Alaric when they cast it into the waters of the

Busento, in Lower Italy. They told the Indians, however, to quiet them, that the much-dreaded child of the sun, Soto, had only gone on a short journey to Heaven, whence he would soon return.

The memory of Soto is still preserved amongst the inhabitants of the southern states of the American Union. The dykes and walls of earth, which are frequently found scattered about in that country, are called to this day "Soto encampments." And many of the rivers, places, and districts, and even the Appalachian mountains, bear the same names in our geographies as those which Soto first made known and were used in the history of his remarkable march.

Soto's successor, Moscoso, now began his preparations for taking over the rest of the army, about three hundred and fifty Spaniards and some forty horses, to the colonies. After an unsuccessful attempt to work their way westward through the prairies of Texas, he decided to go down the Mississippi to the Gulf of Mexico, and to build vessels to accomplish this purpose. The old musket barrels and other iron that they had still remaining were turned into axes, saws, nails, and anchors. Wood was cut and kept in store in their winter quarters (1542). Of the Indians they bought a quantity of cloaks and other stuffs made of a plant of the genus malva. Their old cloaks were used for calking, and the new ones were sewed together to make sails. Of the same plant as the natives made their cloaks, and which grew in profusion in the swamps of the Mississippi, they manufactured the necessary ropes; and thus, after a great deal of trouble, they managed to complete seven small brigantines. The horses were slaughtered and their flesh dried, and the voyage down the stream was commenced.

But scarcely had the retreat begun, than the people of the country rose like a lion when he sees his hunter taking to flight. If the Spaniards had been unable to find a Montezuma, an avenging Guatimozin, however, was upon their heels. A young, warlike, and patriotic cazique of the valley of the Mississippi, named Quigual-tan-gui, was at the head of all the tribes which had conspired to pursue the Spaniards. The Mississippi swarmed with a fleet of canoes, painted red, yellow, and blue, which followed the fugitives day and night, causing them great sufferings.

Fighting continually, and experiencing many serious losses, Moscoso at length reached the delta and the mouth of the Mississippi. As he put to sea, the Indians sent forth terrible yells of triumph, considering themselves the victors. After a long and dangerous voyage along the coast, the remainder of the Spaniards, clothed in the skins of animals and covered with scars, at length, in the autumn of 1543, reached their countrymen in Mexico.

For four years no news had been received there of this once splendid expedition. In vain had the regent of Cuba, Doña Isabella—as the wife of Cortez had done under similar circumstances—sent out ships every year to search for her husband. The commanders of these vessels looked for signs of him everywhere along the far-stretching coast of Florida, and they even went as far as " Bacallaos" (Newfoundland), affixing on the trees, near all the harbours and bays where they landed, letters and other tokens for Soto.

But, as we have said, it had been all in vain, and when Doña Isabella had learnt where her husband had found his last resting-place, as a young and mourning widow, she returned to Spain. The Mississippi now fell into forgetfulness. After this disastrous expedition of Soto, and the knowledge that he had even frequently experienced deep falls of snow in his winter encampments, the Spaniards became aware that there was nothing for them in the north. "IN THE SOUTH, IN THE SOUTH, there is our happiness," was more than ever the ruling idea.

For the next hundred years no Spaniard, and indeed no European, saw the Mississippi again. The extreme points of the delta, formed of the mud and wood refuse of the river, which, like long tongues of land stretch out far into the sea, may at the utmost have been yearly sighted by the Spanish silver fleets when following the course laid down for them along the northern portion of the Gulf of Mexico. But when they beheld these tongues, the Spaniards would scarcely have thought of the grand river of Florida, in the bed of which the great conqueror, Fernando de Soto, lay buried. They called them merely "*el Cabo de Lodo*" (the dirt or morass cape).

In truth, a name of meaning, for it tells plainly enough the reason why the discovery of the Mississippi proceeded so slowly. All the other great streams of America, the St. Lawrence, the Orinoco, the Amazon, the La Plata, meet the sea in broad and deep bays, which cut far into the land, and of themselves invite all navigators, so to speak, to enter and sail up them. They all open their mouths like a trumpet, whilst the Mississippi closes its mouths almost like an oyster.

A few decades after the death of Columbus, therefore, all these rivers were not only discovered, but sea-ships sailed up and down them. But the Mississippi ending in "dirt and morass capes," led no one into it of itself. And this, the most important river of the new world, which now sees more vessels floating in its waters than all the others put together, long continued a book with seven seals.

To the above cause it is owing that the Mississippi, at last, was not, like the other rivers, opened to Europe by vessels entering up it from the sea, but rather by its having been navigated downwards, from its source to the ocean. One hundred and thirty years after the Indians had chased the remnant of Soto's warriors out of the mouth of this river, the small bark was carried to a point, not far removed from its source, which was destined to float down its whole length, and thus make it known to the world.

In studying the history of discovery, it is particularly interesting to find out how events have followed just in such a way as the nature of things, the character of the countries and the seas necessarily developed them. This study enables us to see that many things are providentially connected, both as to time and place, which at first sight appear accidental. For the most part this fact may be proved in detail; but I must be content here with pointing to it in a general way. What I wish to assert is, that the history of discovery in a manner may be compared to the growth of a flower: that everything has progressed, become developed, and has branched out of a certain necessity.

The man who directed the rudder of that little bark, which, as I have said, floated down the Mississippi almost from its source, was Father Marquette, a member of the, at that time in America, and indeed everywhere, so powerful order of the Jesuits.

I cannot here mention for the second time this wonderful order, without doing that which I ought, perhaps, to have done long ago, calling attention to the extraordinary energy which its members from the first displayed in the discovery of the new world.

This order was founded just at the time when the work of the discovery was in full progress. Scarcely was the society formed, than the first idea of its members was to draw the new world into the bond of Christian faith, to establish a universal moral community, and thus to gain the fulfilment of the unity promised by the prophets.

Even the personal scholars, envoys, and contemporaries of Loyola went on board the ships of the Portuguese, and sailed with them to the east; and also on board the ships of the Spaniards and French, and sailed with them to the West.

In the Orient, particularly in Japan, China, and the Moluccas, they penetrated further, and acquired a more intimate knowledge of things than any Europeans had done before them; they built up with wonderful rapidity a far-spread Christian church, though open to the objection that it was set up far too quickly to last. But in the West, the greatest field for their activity awaited them. They not only followed the Spanish ships, but when they got to the new world, they placed themselves everywhere at the head. They extended their explorations into the most distant corners, as well into the thick pine forests of Canada, where the ice seldom melts, as into the primeval woods of the tropics, where the air is ever hot and suffocating.

They sought out the American savages in their hiding-places, not with the terror of the sword, but unarmed, with the cross and the hymns of their church, which the barbarians found so fascinating and irresistible that it has been said the Jesuists had become possessed of the lute of Orpheus, by means of which they had brought peace into the wilderness, and made the wolves their servants

Yet they were often torn to pieces by these scarcely tamed wolves, for such is the fickle nature of the Indians, that occasionally they will rise against their benefactors. As early as the year 1569, scarcely twenty years after the arrival in Canada of the first Jesuits, the Indians had enriched the society's calendar of martyrs by more than fifty that had suffered death in their cause, and been placed amongst the saints. But the fathers always came back in all mildness to their children, to continue the work which they had begun.

Amongst a long list of names registered in the culture-history of the new world, we may cite: Anchieta, the Thaumaturgus (worker of miracles) of the new world; Almeida, a born Englishman, now, his reverers say, an angel; and Robrega, surnamed "the father of the children of the forest." Men such as these put a stop to the long-standing bloody feuds of the Red Skins, to that war of all against all, and in Paraguay, as well as on the Amazons and at the feet of the Andes, they were the first to sound the bell of peace in the little chapels which, with their own hands, they had erected.

When the Jesuits obtained greater power and means, they by degrees transformed their little chapels into splendid large churches and colleges; and as they alone adopted a sound system, by means of which the Indians could be brought together, and, if not civilised, at least tamed, their little Indian missions in the course of time grew into powerful Indian states, in which these people were ensured as great a degree of civil order and freedom as their wild nature seems to be capable of.

Throughout America the Jesuits have been the champions of Indian freedom, and as such they have frequently experienced quite as much, or even more, persecution from their own countrymen as from the barbarians. At the head of the latter they have at times retired into the wilderness, far from the slavery-loving colonists, the so-called Christians, that they might preserve the freedom of their adoptive children, and form communities suited to their requirements. And these benevolent doings have not been destined to end, as all the earlier and latter attempts to civilise the red races have ended—in their destruction.

The missionaries and discoverers whom the order of the Jesuits sent forth were for the most part not only possessed of the courage of martyrs, and of statesman-like-qualities, but likewise (and this is here particularly worthy of note) of great knowledge and learning. They were enthusiastic travellers, naturalists, and geographers; they were the best mathematicians and astronomers of their time. They have been the first to give us faithful and circumstantial accounts of the new lands and peoples they visited. There are few districts in the interior of America concerning which the Jesuits have not supplied us with the oldest and best works. We can scarcely attempt the study of any American language without meeting with a grammar compiled by a Jesuit.

In addition to their chapels and colleges in the wilderness, the Jesuits likewise erected observatories; and there are few rivers, lakes, and mountains in the interior, which they have not been the first to draw upon our maps.

There was a time when the general of the order of Jesuits in Rome, into whose hands maps, reports, and grammars streamed from all parts of the globe, must have been the best informed man in the world. He stood at the head of a realm—greater than the empire of the Macedonians and Romans—which conquered with the breviary, the rosary, and the songs of the Church; which, with its many arms, embraced the whole globe, and whose envoys and servants penetrated as well into the secret cabinets of emperors and kings, as to the hidden sources of the streams and waters of the old and new worlds.

"Who can read the history of the Jesuits outside of Europe, without a certain, to be sure divided, admiration? What skill have they not everywhere displayed! What a spirit in the finding and adaptation of means! What science in turning every item of knowledge to account! What a courage of self-denial! What heroism in individuals! Patience, fervour, and dauntlessness cannot be carried further than the Jesuits have carried these virtues!"

In a work written AGAINST THE JESUITS, a distinguished French author, where he comes to speak of the activity of this order in Asia, breaks out in the foregoing words. In us, who have here to occupy ourselves with the history of geography in America, where we can learn so much more of them than in Asia, a little scientific sympathy for the JESUITS were still more pardonable, although, in our enmity and war against JESUITISM, we do not yield to that Frenchman in the least.

But I now return to that little barque, which, as already said, at the end of the seventeenth century floated down the Mississippi, carrying a Jesuit in it, and which has led me to these somewhat lengthy, though I trust not inappropriate, remarks.

The French Jesuits, as related in the foregoing chapter, had already reached and explored the western corner of the great lakes of the St. Lawrence system. They had there heard, from the Algonquin tribes dwelling in those districts, of a great river which flowed in the rear of those lakes, and which they called Missepi, or Metschasepi, or Mississippi—that is, the father of waters.

The fame of this river was already spread, in particular amongst the people on lake Michigan (or as it was then called, *Lac des Illinois*), and from times far back the Indians had been accustomed, on their hunting and war excursions, to carry their canoes from the tributaries of that lake, across the present state of Wisconsin, to the waters of the Mississippi. These historic facts point out the way which the French discoverers were necessarily led to follow.

The last cross planted by the Jesuits stood at that time at the source of the so-called little Fox River, which flows into lake Michigan, exactly on the border of the watershed of the two great systems, the St. Lawrence and the Mississippi. On the other side of this cross, was the Mesconsin flowing towards the Mississippi. The name of this river, afterwards changed into "Wisconsin," has become celebrated as the appellation of a state. It was here that the missionary Marquette, full of desire to extend the rule of the cross, and to convert the people on "the father of rivers," in the month of May, 1673, commenced his remarkable journey of discovery. He had as companions, the Sieur Jolliet, a citizen of Quebec, a man of great energy, and five experienced French fur-hunters. In two barque canoes, these Mississippi discoverers glided down the Wisconsin river, amidst its numerous fishes and birds.

The scenery they passed through resembled that of a beautiful park. But the accounts which the natives gave them of the west were not inviting.

The latter were astonished when they heard what these few Frenchmen were about to undertake, and they did their best to dissuade them from the pursuance of their plan. They told them it was extremely difficult to navigate the great river; that it was full of monsters that devoured both men and canoes. At one place, they said, there was a gigantic demon whose roaring could be heard at a great distance, and who cast all who came near him into an abyss; and the country, moreover, was full of roving bands of warriors, from whom the worst was to be feared. These descriptions probably had reference, on the one hand, to the beautiful and celebrated St. Anthony Cataract, on the Upper Mississippi;

and on the other, to the tribe of Sioux Indians, who, although the relators had reason to fear them, were not the enemies of Europeans.

Father Marquette, who was the soul of the undertaking, told the friendly Indians, however, that he had a highly important mission to the west, for it was to spread there the knowledge of the true God. In this cause, if necessary, he was ready and willing to sacrifice his life. But he would be on his guard against demons and bands of warriors, and he hoped to avoid injury from either.

As they floated upon the clear waters of the Wisconsin, Father Marquette and his companions were led through flowery and fertile pastures and woodlands, close by islands and hills covered with beautiful trees, from which hung festoons of wild vines. Numbers of deer and wild cows broused beneath oak and walnut trees. The voyage was in every way prosperous, and about five weeks after their departure from Lake Michigan, they glided out of the Wisconsin into the great Father of Waters, whose waves, here crystal bright, rolled between banks of great beauty to the south.

At this sight, says father Marquette in his journal—a few rare copies of which still exist—their joy was great. They took the geographical latitude of these points tolerably correctly, and gave themselves up to the smoothly and still southward flowing stream.

They went down the river for about sixty leagues without seeing anything but large herds of buffaloes, and great quantities of various other animals and birds, extensive pastures on the one shore, hills and mountains of many forms on the other. Now and then they landed, made a fire and cooked their dinner, returning, however, soon to their canoes, for fear of being surprised by enemies; and by night they always cast anchor, and slept as far as possible from land.

At last, after a pleasant voyage of eight days' duration, they saw the first signs of inhabitants, in a well-trodden path, and soon afterwards an Indian village of the tribe of the Illinois.

These people received the strangers in a friendly way offering them the pipe of peace. Marquette found that the French were as well known by report to the inhabitants of the Mississippi, as this river itself for some time past had been known to the French. He discovered, too, that European articles of trade had preceded the Frenchmen. He saw French clothes and iron utensils. He even found European firelocks in use, which had come thus far by the intervention of other tribes. But this was only the case on the eastern banks of the Mississippi. The people on the western bank knew nothing of the Europeans, of their fabrics, and especially nothing of their powder and guns, with the ·thunder of which their neighbours on the eastern bank kept them in a state of surprise and alarm.

It is a most interesting fact, everywhere repeated in America, that the goods and even the animals of Europeans, and with them many of their habits and customs, became known to the Indians before they saw the Europeans themselves. A similar phenomenon, as is known, was observed amongst our old German ancestors in the times of the Roman Empire, for then both Roman coins and goods had been carried by Mercury much further than Mars had transported his cohorts.

Father Marquette made particular inquiries of these people about the nature of the river he had discovered, and the direction of its course. He, however, could learn nothing more than that it sprang from several lakes amongst the nations far up in the north; how far it had to flow, and into what sea it poured, they could not tell.

At first Marquette was in much doubt on the latter point. His mind fluctuated between three probable seas. At one time he thought the river would turn to the west, and empty itself into the Gulf of California, or into the South Sea. Then he fancied it might take an easterly direction, and flow into one of the rivers which the English had discovered on the coast of Virginia, the size and the sources of which, however, were unknown to them.

At last he came to think that the river might continue to flow to the south and pour into the Gulf of Mexico. It does not appear that Father Marquette was acquainted with the Spanish reports of the expedition of Soto into the countries of the Mississippi. They are never mentioned at all in his memoirs.

Until the end of June, he and his companions remained with the Illinois, with whom they continued on friendly terms, receiving from them much assistance for the prosecution of their voyage. The course of the Mississippi continued southwards, and they floated peacefully down its beautiful clear waters.

But this pleasant voyage was suddenly interrupted on arriving at a point where another exceedingly rapid and turbid river rushed into the Mississippi. It was a great mass of water in which floated many trees and bushes; indeed, whole islands, and the noise it made was almost like that of a waterfall. It was the wild Missouri, called, however, by the natives, according to Marquette, the Pekitanoni.

We find this name used in French books and maps for forty or fifty years afterwards. Yet in the map made by Marquette, we see the name Missouri put down, though only to designate an Indian village or tribe. From these Missouri Indians in the neighbourhood of the confluence of the rivers, with whom the French soon had much intercourse, the name of the stream, "*la Rivière des Missouris*," was derived. Marquette perceived that this great river came from the west, in which direction, according to one of his suppositions, the Mississippi was to flow.

He probably now came to the conclusion that the continent must extend very far towards the west, and the South Sea be a great distance off. He would further have concluded that the intermediate land could not slope down towards the ocean, but rather that it must rise to a great height. He gathered, too, from the natives, that the Pekitanoni came from countries very remote. All this confirmed his opinion that the Mississippi emptied itself into the Gulf of Mexico.

He heard likewise from the Indians that there was another river beyond the sources of the Missouri, which river flowed in a westerly direction and poured into a sea. This sea, he thought, must be the South Sea. He formed the resolution, if God in His grace should grant him health, at a later period to extend his discoveries in that direction. He had no conception of the great difficulties in the way of such an undertaking, and that not till one hundred and forty years after his time, two bold Europeans, the celebrated Lewis and Clark, the explorers of the Missouri, would succeed in carrying out his plan.

Meanwhile, he continued his voyage southwards, and in a few days, after passing between romantic rocky scenery, he reached a part where another large tributary joined the Mississippi from the east. The children of the country called it Wabous-Kigou (the river Wabous). Without doubt it was the river which the French later called Wabash, and the principal channel of which subsequently received the name of Ohio, *i.e.* the beautiful river, the name Wabash continuing to be applied only to one of its branches. The course of the Ohio, which river the natives told him came from the east, from countries inhabited by neighbours and enemies of the Iroquois, would now have put an end to Marquette's hypothesis, that the Mississippi might turn to the east and fall into the Atlantic ocean on the coasts of Virginia or Florida. Such a vast stream of water coming from that quarter proved that there must be mountains between the Mississippi and the sea.

Further down the river, below the confluence of the Ohio, Marquette found that the inhabitants on the left banks were possessed of iron instruments, of hatchets, knives, and even of guns and powder and shot, although since Soto's time no European could ever have approached their country. They told him that they procured these things from the east, through the intervention of Europeans in that direction—without doubt of the English settlers in Virginia. At that time the English had not crossed the Alleghany Mountains, yet articles of their manufacture had everywhere preceded them as far as the Mississippi.

From the other side, from the west and south-west, similar forerunners of the Europeans likewise appeared to have reached the Mississippi from Mexico. Father Marquette speaks of Indian nations possessing horses. This is not to be otherwise explained than that some of the wild horses of Mexico, descendants of the races introduced by the Spaniards, had already wandered across the prairies to the west as far as the Mississippi. Thus things introduced by the Spaniards as well as by the Anglo-Saxons met at that river long before the interests and the arms of these two peoples came in conflict.

Marquette and his companions always took with them the "calumet," the pipe of peace, which the Illinois Indians had made them a present of, and they always held it up to the inhabitants of the river district in proof that they had none but peaceful intentions. At times they came into situations of great danger, but the calumet and their breviary, their religious songs, and their general quiet appearance, helped them over difficulties.

It was of great use to Father Marquette that he could speak six Indian languages, and amongst them the

Illinois, which was understood far down the river. At a point considerably to the south, they again met with a great river and an Indian village called "Akamsa." This word, without doubt, was subsequently altered into Arkansas, the name now in use for the great tributary of the Mississippi which comes from the Rocky Mountains in the west.

Aided by the people whom he met here, who understood Illinois, Marquette imparted to them some knowledge of the mysteries of the Christian faith. "He was not certain," he said "whether they understood what he told them about Heaven; but it was a scattering of the good seed, which at some day might bear fruit."

He may have been the more disposed to believe this, as the Arkansas Indians were extremely friendly and willing to serve him. They prepared sacrifices, and slaughtered dogs for him every day. He found them, too, acquainted with agriculture, and Indian corn much in use, just as Soto had formerly experienced on the Mississippi. But Marquette heard no traditions of that warlike leader, who, however, had been everywhere about in these districts, and who must have left impressions behind him so totally different from those made by Marquette with his religious usages and peaceful companions. The Arkansas people informed him that he had still ten days' journey to the sea, and that the river continued as hitherto to flow on to the south. They did not know the nations which lived at the end of the river, as they were separated from them by others who were their enemies. Marquette was now quite convinced that the river could flow into no other sea than the Gulf of Mexico, from which he believed himself to be distant only one and a half degrees of latitude.

To solve this problem appears to have been considered as the main purpose of the expedition, and that it had now been accomplished without going down to the sea. Besides, Marquette thought it would be extremely dangerous to penetrate as far as the gulf, not so much on account of the hostile Indians, as of the Europeans. The Indians he had previously met with had been described to him as dangerous enemies, and yet he had always managed to get on with them in a friendly way. But with the Spaniards, whose power extended all over the Gulf of Mexico, it would be quite a different thing, for they considered all the lands to the north of that gulf as having been discovered by, and as belonging to them; as conquered and watered by the blood of their forefathers, and as bestowed upon them, moreover, by the head of the Church.

On the shores of that gulf, Marquette expected to meet with Spanish settlements, or at least with Spanish ships. In this case his fate would have been sad, for the

Spaniards looked upon all other discoverers in America with jealousy and hate. Had Marquette fallen in with any of that nation, he would probably have been imprisoned for life, and all the advantages of his discovery would have been lost. The Spaniards even hid from the world their own discoveries; how much more would this be the case in respect to those made by foreigners.

At the confluence of the Arkansas and Mississippi, the little party of French explorers held a council, and decided to return to the north. On the 17th of July, therefore, they left their southern *non plus ultrà*, and commenced their dangerous and tedious voyage in their little canoes against the current of the Mississippi.

On their passage up the stream they discovered, a little above the point where the Missouri pours into the Mississippi, another river coming from the north-east — called now the Illinois. Inquiries of the natives, and his own reflection, brought Marquette to the conclusion that this river would lead him by a more direct way than the Wisconsin to Lake Michigan. He took with him one of the native chiefs, who was well acquainted with the navigation and the nature of the stream, and arrived at last at the southern shores of the lake near to which is the source of the Illinois.

Those extensive, beautiful, and fertile lands, forming the great state of Illinois of the present day, Marquette was therefore the first European to travel through in their whole length, and likewise to describe. "Never," he says, "have I seen anything to surpass these districts in excellence of soil, of pastures, of wood, and also in the abundance of game—of deer, stags, birds, swans, ducks, and even of beavers." In the autumn of the year 1673, he reached Lake Michigan, from which he had departed in the spring, at a point near to where the present large and flourishing commercial city of Chicago is situated. Soon afterwards, however, he suffered the death of a martyr, falling under the tomahawk of a wild Canadian. HIS BONES were buried in the neighbourhood of the sources of the Mississippi; SOTO'S, inclosed in an oak-tree, were sunk in the central part of the river; and THOSE OF NAVAEZ left to bleach at the bottom of the sea in front of the Mississippi delta.

The French fur-hunters and adventurers now soon followed in the steps of their countryman, subjugated the Mississippi regions, and gradually explored the greater part of its tributaries. In the course of the eighteenth century many small settlements were established by the French on the bluffs of the river, and then it was made over by them to the Spaniards. But at the beginning of the nineteenth century it came again into the hands of the French. It was as if a game at ball was being played with the Titan river—and Napoleon at length, tired of the game, sold the Mississippi with all belonging to it—like Esau his birthright for a mess of porridge—for a few million dollars to the United States.

And these citizens of the United States have flooded the river districts with population. In a short time they have poured eight million "workmen" into its valleys and branches, and, as if by magic, have called into life large and beautiful towns and harbours, in which fleets of gigantic steamers are gathered together, like swans upon our pools. Under their hands the wild natural park of the Mississippi has been turned into a garden of Ceres and Pomona. Artificial vineyards flourish upon the shores, and the river of the savage Sioux and the barbarous Choctaws begins to contest the palm with Father Rhine. And, lastly, they have explored its furthest reaching arms and sources in the Rocky Mountains, and have worked their way up them, and to the South Sea, where in all haste they have laid the foundation of a new great state.

CHAPTER IV.

THE MARCH OF THE RUSSIANS AND COSSACKS THROUGH SIBERIA TO AMERICA.

Annika Stroganoff sends his People over the Ural (anno 1570)—Jermak Timofejeff and his Cossacks ride over the Ural (1578)—Jermak gains Possession of "Sibir" (1580)—The Cossacks reach the Lena (1628)—The Cossacks gain Possession of Kamtschatka (1690-1706)—The Cossacks hear of the "Great Land," (America) (1706)—Peter the Great orders the Discovery of the "Great Land," (North-West America) (1723)—Behring and Tschirokoff reach America from Siberia (1741)—The Russians take Possession of North-West America (1760).

At the beginning of the eighteenth century, nearly all the nations of Europe had shared in the common work of the discovery of America, and colonies from all of them were already established in the new world. Each of them had long taken their part in it: the Spaniards and Portuguese, who had from the first placed themselves at the head of the movements, had had the lion's share; the Dutch, the French, the Britons, who streamed in succession to win the sceptre of the ocean-dominion, had followed in the track of the former, and, in spite of the Papal bull of partition, had laid hold of considerable territories for themselves. The two latter ruled over almost the whole eastern portion of North America, and next to them, in icy Greenland, the small but daring Danish people had fixed themselves. Even the inhabitants of central Europe, the Germans and Italians, had many times made their appearance on the further side of the Atlantic Ocean, either on their own account, or in the train of other nations, as useful colonists, expert admirals, and scientific discoverers.

But that, finally, even those who dwell in the extreme east of our continent, the Russians, should have found their way to America, may justly be regarded with astonishment. For they are not only the furthest distant of all the Europeans in a direct line from the main body of America (a meridian drawn through the centre of America goes through the centre of Russia in Europe), but they appear also to be hopelessly separated by a wide expanse of immeasurable desert. Nevertheless, their Cossacks have found their way through the labyrinth of Siberian wastes to America, and have, by their own exertion and in their own way, brought to pass a new and especial discovery of the new world. To all the other nations of Europe, Columbus showed the way; but the enterprises of the Russians had nothing to do with Columbus. All the other nations spread the SAIL and reached the new world by the WATERY OCEAN PATH; the Russians alone mounted on horseback and opened the OVERLAND ROUTE. They made, in fact, a RIDE ROUND THE WORLD. All the other nations followed the sun from the east to the land of the west; the Russians alone arrived there from the west and rode to meet the sun, and their migration was exactly opposed to the universal direction of civilisation and colonisation, from Southern Asia across Europe, towards America. Working onwards through the whole of Northern Asia in a wonderfully rapid course of conquest, they arrived in a short time at the shores of the Pacific Ocean, and there produced their own Columbus, who established their claim on the Siberia of America. In a scientific point of view, the merit belongs to them of having solved the problem which so long occupied the navigators and the learned men of Europe, the question whether, and how, the two great divisions of the dry portion of the earth's surface were united with, or separated from, each other. In a political point of view, the appearance of the Russians in the North American seas was a new phenomenon with manifold results of importance, and whose development goes on increasing even at the present day.

The remarkable expedition, at once of discovery and of conquest, made by the Russians and Cossacks, which was to lead them across the Pacific Ocean, took its rise on the shores of the Black and Caspian Seas. And it is sufficiently remarkable that the first impulse to this movement, as to those of the Spaniards and Portuguese, should have been given by the strife of Christendom with Islam. About the middle of the sixteenth century the Russian empire, after the conquest of the Tartar principalities of Kasan and Astrachan, had a tolerably extensive circumference. In the east, it was bounded by the long chain of the Ural Mountains separating Europe and Asia. These mountains were for a long time the Pyrenees of the Russians. Already, in earlier times, they had crossed these Pyrenees for trade and for warfare, though they had never acquired a permanent influence over their neighbours in the east. The first beginning was made by the speculating procedures of the now well-known family of Count Stroganoff.

A certain Annika Stroganoff, who is regarded as the ancestor of this family, had set up salt works in the Ural, in the land of the Sisenes, and people from the east resorted to him to exchange costly furs with salt. These furs, the hide of the little animal which the Russians name "Sobol," (sable), were the object that allured the Europeans across the Ural. It was these same sable furs, which are exclusively peculiar to the country of Siberia, that led them further, through the whole of Northern Asia, through the forests from land to land. The whole conquest of Siberia might be named a chase of the sable, pursued for a hundred years half round the globe.

It was to buy sables that Annika Stroganoff first sent his people across the Ural Mountains, and thus they came as peaceable traders as far as the great river Ob. As by these speculations they brought about great advantages to the empire, the Czars bestowed on the Stroganoffs large districts on the Kama in the western part of the Ural, which they provided with colonies and towns, and by the possession of these, became chieftains of great power.

In the year 1578, the grandson of the first Stroganoff received a visit from a Cossack chieftain, by name Jermak Timofejeff, who with his followers had, in Cossack fashion, led a life of war, the life at once of a robber and a hero, in Southern Russia, and was now in flight from the powerful hostility of the Czar Ivan Vasiljevitsch II. The Cossacks fled from the powerful state now forming in Russia, as once the Norwegian Jarls of the ninth century before the kingdom established in Scandinavia, and in like manner, and in consequence of a similar occasion, did their nation increase in power and greatness.

Jermak had with him some thousands of mounted followers, and his host Stroganoff, who feared these Cossack robber knights, told them of the lands in the east, and of the rivers which led thither, and which his people had discovered in the course of their travels.

Jermak and his followers, led by the guides of Stroganoff, passed in the year of 1578, across the Ural, going up the valley of the river Tschussovaja, and then downward along other rivers to the great Ob. They found there a little Tartar sovereignty, a fragment of the great monarchy of Ghengis Khan, such as the sovereignties of Kasan, Astrachan, and Crim had been, and whose chief city "Sibir" lay in the centre of the region of the Ob, in the country where now stands the great Siberian capital, Tobolsk, on the Irtish.

That world-defying, courageous spirit which Ghengis Khan and Tamerlane had once breathed into the Tartars, had long been quenched. Their little kingdom, in which cattle-breeding, the chase, and traffic were pursued, still existed only because they had as yet found no powerful enemy.

The Cossacks, on the contrary, were just then in full strength and flower of their national development. They were the young and fresh scholars of the Tartars, against whom they had often served the Muscovites as *avant-garde*. And this body of Jermak's Cossacks, flying from their native country before the wrath of the Czar, must have been especially inspired with the courage of despair. At home, on account of their misdeeds, they had no mercy to expect, and when once they had crossed the Ural, there was no alternative for them save to conquer or die. They attacked thenceforth everywhere with the greatest bravery the superior power of the Siberian Tartars, and at last, after many a battle and skirmish, gained possession of their capital city, in which Jermak, after three years' campaign, established himself as its commandant. Meanwhile, as his little force of adherents had greatly melted away with these combats and exertions, he could not expect to be able to maintain himself with these alone in the sovereignty of his new possessions; but, on the other hand, he might well hope that after so praiseworthy and promising a feat he might meet with favour in his own country. He therefore made a virtue of necessity, and sent to his Muscovite Czar a rich selection of sable fur, and the tidings that he had conquered for him the kingdom of Kutschum Chans, Sibir on the Ob, that he laid it all at the feet of his liege lord, and besought him, therefore, for confirmation of his post, and a despatch of reinforcements.

Both were granted, and thus was Russia thrown into a career of discovery and conquest, which, beginning with Northern Asia, was, as we have said, to reach to China, the Pacific Ocean, and America.

The name Sibir, which at first was attached only to a town, a small principality on the Irtish, received a wider signification the further the conquerors went, till at last it distinguished nearly the half of one of the quarters of the globe. In spite of its size, Siberia is yet a very uniform country, confined by the sameness of its characteristics to a strict geographical and historical unity. Bounded on the north by the Frozen Ocean, on the west by the Ural, on the south by the gigantic mountain range of Central Asia, it exhibits within these limits the same colossal level flat, stretching from east to west, and has everywhere the same products, the same plants and animals. In short, almost throughout, communication and traffic meet the same advantages and the same difficulties.

In the eastern direction no confining mountain walls arise; but a crowd of streams, which interweave the whole land and belong to the greatest and fairest rivers of the world, stretch their arms, so to speak, towards each other in the midst of the plain. They are all navigable, mostly without cataracts, and approach each other so closely with their sources and tributaries, that from one to the other only small isthmuses are formed, over which goods have to be carried. These isthmuses, named by the Russians "woloks," once passed over, and other river districts reached, an uninterrupted far-extending voyage in all directions may be undertaken.

In the whole of the old world there is scarcely another

net of navigable streams so large and so closely interwoven as this of Siberia. On account of the likeness of these streams, which ALL spring in Central Asia, and ALL towards the north, fall into the so-called "Tunds" (ice-morasses) of the Polar Sea, the same mode of navigation is alike available for all. The same form of boats prevails through the whole of Siberia; also the same sledges, the same beasts of burden or draught, are made use of in the whole country. The peoples of the lands, although distinct in race and speech, had, even from ancient times, a great uniformity of customs, usages, and social economy. Their discoverer, or conqueror, had no strange modes of cultivation to study, no new arts to learn. Everywhere are the same half-nomads, taming the reindeer, hunting with dogs, riding on horses, armed with bows and arrows. Hence we may see how natural it was that an enemy of superior force, if once he came from the west across the Ural Mountains, and coveted the possession of this country, should grasp the whole from river to river, and scarcely stop, save before the mountains in the south, the ice in the north, and the great ocean in the east.

The Cossacks were, in truth, such an antagonist to the Siberian races. They were, so to speak, born, brought up, and trained for the conquest of Siberia. Their own European country, in which their schooling had been passed, was in many respects like the Siberian regions. It was, like them, flat, cold, abounding in snow and steppes, and had a network of streams of similar character. From the earliest times the Cossacks constructed river boats and sledges of a like kind, and were accustomed to mount their horses, now to take to their barks, and thus transform themselves from horsemen to sailors, from sailors to horsemen. With their wretched river boats they had in earlier times accomplished the boldest expeditions up and down the river, and over the stormy Euxine to Asia Minor and Constantinople.

Their race of horses also, bred in the steppes of southern Asia, were, so to say, made for the conquest of Siberia. These creatures are small, light, and agile, as is suited to such far-extending plains, where the stages and daily marches must be long. Like their masters, they were accustomed to hunger, thirst, cold, and the endurance of great fatigues, and knew, like the chamois, how to scrape their scanty nourishment out of the snow. When grass was wanting, they devoured fish, as the Icelanders do.

Moreover, their acquaintance with the later European kind of arms—with iron, guns, powder, and shot—gave the Cossacks no small superiority over the native children of Siberia. As regarded weapons of war, the Tungouses, the Yakoutes, Buriates, and Mongols were still on the footing of Tamerlane's soldiers. They had only bows and arrows, and the greater part of them were as unacquainted with iron as the American Indians. The Cossacks commonly carried with them some small cannon or carronades, whose fire-breathing mouths raised among these nomad hordes as great a panic, and gave to the Cossacks as great a superiority in war, as was the case with the Mexicans and their subjugators the Spaniards.

In like manner as the physical nature and training, were the moral characteristics, the political customs, and the usages of the Cossacks in a high degree appropriate to an undertaking of the kind proposed. All Siberia was full, so to speak, of men living solitarily, of many small scattered tribes and peoples. It was, therefore, necessary to divide beforehand the forces of the invaders; small bodies of troops had to be distributed everywhere; many a time they had to make a dozen warriors suffice to subjugate and keep in check a whole tribe; often some hundreds only could be spared for the occupation of a river-territory or a kingdom. It follows, of course, that for this there would be need not so much of large, well-disciplined armies, trained to mechanical obedience, as of light troops in many divisions, easily moved, skilful, and self-acting.

The Cossacks, whose name originally signifies freemen, had developed in themselves a kind of republican constitution, a sort of self-government—of course only after

Cossack fashion. With them all were equal by birth, as is customary among robbers. The councils were held by all and in the presence of all, and each one might freely express his opinion. They chose themselves their superiors, their "hetmans" and "sotniks," and they obeyed them when they saw that they tended to the good of the community. But at times they deposed their leaders, and placed others from amongst themselves at their head.

Thus was every one accustomed to be himself either lord or servant, according as circumstances required of him. Thus have we often seen Cossacks of common birth who have placed themselves at the head of a corps and acted as generals; others who were arrayed as ambassadors, and who undertook and executed diplomatic missions to some Mongol or Bashkir monarch, or even to the Emperor of China. The greatness of their undertakings, the zeal for discovery and conquest which had been awakened in them, the passion for the acquisition of land,—all these things filled the common Cossacks with a like heroism, and aroused their faculties in a like manner, as had been the case with the Almagros, Pizarros, and other leaders of the Spaniards, who could not read or write, and yet conquered and governed empires.

The first river-territory that the Cossacks reached was, as I said, that of the Tobol. At the point where its chief streams unite in one powerful artery, they forthwith built their first "ostrog," or, as it was called in America, their first "fort." This, in consequence of the influx of new comers, was gradually transformed into the important city of Tobolsk, which now placed in the centre of the district of the Tobol, speedily became the focus of the population, the head-quarters of the newly organised government, and the starting-point of all more distant enterprises towards the east. From the first, the principal march of the Cossacks and Russians went right through the centre of the whole land of Siberia, equidistant from the gigantic mountain masses of the south and the inhospitable morasses, the frozen "Tunds," and the shores of the polar seas in the north. This line became the principal route of traffic of the country. In this, cutting as it did across the centre of the great river-region, the chief colonies of the country were founded: eastward from Tobolsk, in the territory of the Ob, the city of Tomsk; eastward from this, on the Yenisei, the city Yeniseisk; then Irkoutsk, on the Lena; still more eastward, in the midst of the district of the Lena, Yakutsk; and finally, quite in the east, on the sea-coast, Okhotsk.

These cities grew successively one out of the other, like the sprouts and knobs in the stem of a fir-tree; and for every following river-province the former ones served as *points d'appui* for the several enterprises.

Every time that this train of conquest and immigration arrived at an important line of river, a pause was made. They fixed themselves firmly; they organised their new territories. They built boats, went both up and down the river exploring—down even as far as the Frozen Ocean—and founded even there little settlements, harbours, and towns, but which never became so important as the inland cities, because the Frozen Sea was not so well fitted to attract a brisk commerce from near or far. While, then, they secured the whole line of the river, and made tributary all the Ostiaks, Samojedes, Tungouses, Yakoutes, or whatever people dwelt there at the time, the flood of colonists and hunters had in the mean while begun to pass over, by an adjoining stream, into another river-territory. They had heard of a new large river in the east, a new nation, a new, yet unexplored region for the chase and for sable-trapping. The Cossacks themselves were a light troop, but they were preceded by a still lighter, more flying *avant-garde*, the so-called "Promischlenniks." These were certain freebooters who hunted on their own account, and at their own risk, whom no one could control, who swarmed everywhere in the woods, housing amidst morasses prowled over by wild beasts, and in this manner preceded the regular body of Cossacks. The "Promischlenniks" had made all the first discoveries in Siberia, and brought home the earliest tidings of everything new. From them the waivodes and hetmans of the Cossacks received the first information when a new expedition was in readiness, or an enterprise ripe for execution. They served the regular soldiers and the officially appointed explorers as pioneers; and even to them a parallel is found in the history of American discovery, in the "*coureur des bois*" of the French, the beaver-trappers of the English, and the Paulists of the Portuguese, who on that condition served in like manner the leaders of great expeditions as forerunners, guides, and skirmishers.

In the manner we have portrayed, the Cossacks had already discovered the "Joandesi," or "Yenisei," the most mighty central river of Siberia, which intersects the whole country in the middle with a wide fork, and cuts it into the two halves of Eastern and Western Siberia. Here they heard, in the beginning of the seventeenth century, of the existence of another river in the east—the mighty Lena—and in the spring of the year 1628, ten of them strapped on their snow-shoes, and sped across into this region under the command of their "Desatnik" (that is, a decurion, or commander of ten men) Wasilei Bugor. Arrived at the principal stream, they built a boat and proceeded downward some way. Everywhere among the Yakoutes and Tungouses did these ten Cossacks spread dismay, and everywhere they collected the wonted tribute of sable-skins. In order to hold the people to their oath of dependence, Bugor posted two Cossacks on the centre of the Lena; two, four hundred miles above; and two more, four hundred miles below. In three years he returned to the Yenesei with a rich store of sable-skins to give a report of his expedition. It may be asked whether, even in the history of America, so extensive a conquest was achieved with so small an army, by a general, in fact, in command of ten men. Other, and somewhat larger troops of Cossacks soon followed Bugor, the first conqueror of the Lena. In 1632, a Cossack chieftain, Beketoff, went far down the Lena, and built the first fortified "ostrog" on this river, in the midst of the Yakoutes. This was the so-called "Ostrog of the Yakoutes," out of which arose later the city of Yakoutsk, the capital of all Eastern Siberia, which finally served as the head-quarters for all more distant expeditions from the east to the Frozen Ocean, to the Pacific, and to America.

The Lena, in its upward course, reaches, like the Yenisei, that famous basin of water which lies amidst the Altai mountains, and is named by the surrounding tribes the "Báikal." As the Russians now possessed both lines leading to this basin, they began their remarkable voyages to this lake, which is enclosed in a wide mountainous gap, and which showed them the way to China and to Mantchooria. The captain Curbat Ivanoff was the man to whom belongs the honour of the first successful expedition to Lake Baikal, and who was followed by many others.

This expedition to the Baikal brought the Russians to another world, to half-civilised tribes, to natural scenes rich in wonders, into the region of the Amoor, which falls into the Pacific Ocean, a region renowned for its silver mines. The brilliant accounts given of all this failed not to excite the greatest sensation in the "ostrogs" and "slobodes" of the Siberian Cossacks. Countless "Promischlenniks" banded together under self-chosen commanders. The cities of Yakoutsk, Yeniseisk, and others already scarce sufficiently occupied, became again almost depopulated; to fill up these gaps, other emigrants from Europe followed. All betook themselves on the way to the Baikal, the Amoor, and the silver mines. The poor tribe of the Burates were almost trodden down by them on the way.

A somewhat similar result took place to what we in our days have witnessed in the discovery of the gold-teeming regions of California. The history of the discovery and colonisation of Siberia is rich in movements of this sort, in such chase of treasure, in such passionate popular wanderings towards delusive goals—the sources of gold and wells of life—as mark the history of America.

Just at the time when the Russians came to the Amoor, in Northern China, the Mantchoos had completed their conquest of this empire. The Mantchoo forces were thus diverted to the south, and their original home on the Amoor would in consequence be somewhat dispeopled and enfeebled when these unexpected guests from Europe arrived there.

With scarcely a conflict the bands of Cossacks sailed and rowed, so to speak, through the heart of Mantchooria down to the mouth of the river Amoor, stormed Chinese fortresses, subjugated many Mantchoo princes, chased away or subdued the inhabiting tribes, the Daurians, the Gilaks, and other Mongol races. And when at last Chinese forces appeared, the little squadrons of the Cossacks put thousands of imperial soldiers to flight. All this happened about the middle of the seventeenth century. It is true the Russians have been obliged since to yield back the greater part of Mantchooria and the district of the Amoor to ~~Russia~~ *Chi*; but it was in consequence of these expeditions that the cities of Irkutsk (1661), and Nertschinsk (1658) were founded, as also that the whole country of Daurian with its abundance of silver mines has remained to Russia. Moreover, the affairs of Russia and China were from this time closely and permanently connected; and an intercourse of commerce was opened which lasts to this day.

From the mouth of the Amoor the Cossacks reached and navigated (1645) that remarkable sea which till then had been wholly unknown to us Europeans, which forms a side basin of the Pacific Ocean, and is called by the Mantchoos "*Tung Lam*" (the Sea of Tung), by us the Sea of Okhotsk.

Some years before some Cossack hordes, seeking a nearer way out from the Lena, had reached the northern part of this sea. The Lena stretches towards Yakutsk far to the east, and the Tung Sea in the same country to the west. The isthmus between the two pieces of water was very soon traversed on horseback and on snow-shoes, and an "ostrog," which obtained the name of Okhotsk, built on the sea. The city which grew out of this has remained to our times the chief Russian port on this sea.

From the Lena, Siberia extends, gradually narrowing, about one thousand six hundred miles further to the east. The length of the rivers decreases with the breadth of the land, and the mighty Lena is followed by the smaller Yana, Indighirka, Kolyma, and at last, in the furthest corner, by the still more insignificant Anadyr, all diminishing like the strings of a harp. The discovery of these more distant rivers of Siberia began in 1638. Some Cossacks, under the guidance of a certain Busa, reached the Yana by water from the mouth of the Lena, while others, under the Sotnick Ivanoff, on horseback, penetrated to its sources from Yakutsk. Here they heard of the Indighirka, and in the year following they trotted on to this river. The Yukagirs who peopled this country were utterly unacquainted with the Cossack cavalry, and showed more terror of the horses than of the men, just as did the Mexicans at the apparition of Cortez's sixteen Centaurs. Yet among these very people have the Russians established their numerous hordes of horses and cattle, as the Spaniards have done among the Indians of America. Moreover, at the time of the irruption of the Cossacks, Siberia was more densely peopled than now—another trait in common with America—and another parallel is furnished by the fact that in both cases the same disease followed on the steps of the European invaders, the small-pox, which carried off whole tribes in Siberia, as in America. Sixteen Cossacks on the Indighirka took captive the ruling prince of the country. On their neighing steeds they charged his forces, armed only with bows and arrows, entirely vanquishing them

them with great slaughter. In 1640, they had completed the conquest of the whole river, eight hundred miles long.

Forthwith they again pricked up their ears, and listened to tales of new rivers in the east, of the Alaseia, and the Kolyma. Strengthened by additional troops, they proceeded in 1646 to subdue this region also. East of the Kolyma, where Siberia approaches its termination, dwells the valiant and remarkable tribe of the Tschuktchi, whose land, if it did not allure with sables and silver mines, had yet another not less precious article deposited by the revolutions of nature on its shores, and along the banks of the river. This consisted of those remarkable accumulations of fossil ivory, the teeth of a long-perished race of huge animals, the so-named mammoth, or primeval elephant. These had indeed been already discovered in other parts of Siberia, but the largest masses are deposited here in the north along the shores of the land of the Tschuktchi. These precious wares, which had great influence in the conquest of Siberia, and in attracting emigrants to the north, and which even at the present day play an important part in Siberian traffic, are also found in the icy northern regions of America. In 1646, the first expedition in search of mammoths' teeth left the Kolyma for the land of the Tschuktchi. Here the inhabitants related of a new large mountainous land, which lay towards the north pole, and the outline of whose coasts could be seen from time to time from the Siberian continent. This land they said was rich in ivory, and there were the most beautiful teeth heaped up there in high banks and mounds. Many believed that this land was peopled and connected with Nova Zembla in the west, and with America in the east. The Cossacks committed themselves, with a daring which a well-prepared Arctic navigator of our time can scarcely understand, to their fragile "Lotki," or boats, covered with leather and bound together with leather thongs, and sought to reach that promised land of ivory in the north pole. They sailed without compass out into the middle of the ice, and struggled with the icebergs. At times their "Lotkis" were shattered like the Greek ships on the rocks of the Bosphorus, at times they froze up amidst the sea one hundred versts from the shores, and there bade defiance to the winter, in order in the following summer to advance a few steps further. Some of them may have reached that remote northern land; but it is not certain. The voyages thither which had been ventured on in the first passionate ardour of Siberian conquest, appear after this to have gone out of fashion, and the whole "ivory land" of the east to have been utterly forgotten again. It is only in our time that, through the travels of Baron Wrangel, more light has been obtained concerning this land, and that it has been recognised as a chain of large islands of which the largest is now called "New Siberia."

It took longest to unveil that long south-eastern strip of Siberia which we call the peninsula of Kamtschatka. This country, which is about the size and shape of Italy, is surrounded by the ocean, and only connected with the continent by a narrow isthmus. Its southern portion projects six hundred geographical miles from the mainland into the sea. The name of Kamtschatka was known by report in Yakutsk since 1690. Some years later, the first party of riders set out thither under the leadership of the Cossack colonel, Atlassoff, who passes for the actual discoverer and conqueror of Kamtschatka. The Russians found in Kamtschatka Japanese writings, and also some Japanese sailors cast ashore there. This, and the fact related to them by the people, that their land stretched much further still to the south, induced the Russians at first to believe that Kamtschatka reached as far as Japan, and such an extent is given it by the oldest maps which we possess of this land. Like the first Spaniards in Peru and Mexico, the first Russians in Kamtschatka were highly honoured, almost deified, by the natives. The Kamtschatkans did not believe that a human hand could harm them, or that resistance was possible, till the Cossacks, by shedding a comrade's blood, had themselves proved to them that they were mortal. The American Indians, as is known, had a like belief in regard to the companions of Columbus, till undeceived by a similar occurrence to the above.

After many repeated expeditions, after many battles fought with the liberty-loving inhabitants, the Russians, overturning all before them, arrived at last, in the year 1706, at the extreme southern extremity of Kamtschatka, where they saw before them the chain of the little Kourile Islands, the southernmost of which certainly come very near to Japan.

It appeared as if the Cossack lust of conquest and thirst for discovery would never be appeased or restrained. They threw themselves forthwith on the islands of the Kouriles, and opened the way to Japan, like as, earlier, along the Amoor; they had found themselves on the direct way to the Celestial Kingdom. In 1712-1713, a Cossack, by name Iwan Kosirewskoi, who afterwards became a monk, led several expeditions to the Kourile Islands, and sent reports of them to Moscow, which contained a tolerably correct description of their position and natural characteristics as far down as Japan.

Thus did the Russians, after the lapse of a century, full of indescribable toil and exertions, full of warlike enterprises and ravages, reach the extreme end of the old world, that fabulous land of Gog and Magog, in which men, in the latter part of the middle ages, when it was to be found nowhere else, had placed the realm of the imaginary Prester John, and in which, since Herodotus's time, had been located one-legged, or one-eyed, and other strange peoples with dogs' tails or ravens' claws.

They now, at the beginning of the eighteenth century, found themselves on a line of coast more than twelve hundred miles long, opposite the north-west end of America, which here faces Asia. As a matter of course, ere long they proceeded thither, as they had done to China and Japan. The first news which the Russians obtained of the "Great Land" (*Bolschaia Semla*) in the east sounded very uncertain, and had, too, some resemblance to those first indications of regions in the west which Columbus had once collected. Tall stems of firs, and other trees, which did not grow in Kamtschatka, were thrown, from time to time, by the currents from the east on the shores of this peninsula. Numberless flocks of land birds used at times to come thither from the east and then go away again in that direction. Whales would come from the east with harpoons in their backs, such as were not known in Kamtschatka; and from time to time foreign-built boats and other unusual objects were stranded there from the east. At last, it was remarked also that the waves of the sea in the east of Kamtschatka had not so long a swell as in the south on the open ocean, whence it was concluded that this was in fact an inner sea, which must be encompassed in the east by some land, just as it was in the west by Asia. The Tschuktchi were the nearest neighbours to America, and it was not possible that some distinct tidings should not come from them to the Russians of a country in the east, to which, from remotest times, they had been in the habit of crossing over. In their numerous conflicts with them the Russians had, from time to time, taken captive men who wore teeth of the walrus in their lips and spoke a perfectly foreign language. These were Americans, who were either trading friends or prisoners of war of the Asiatics. From these people it would have been heard by many that the "Great Eastern Land" was no island, but a large unlimited territory, with great rivers and full of woods and mountain ranges. Many even maintained that in clear weather this land could at times be descried from the capes on the coast of the country of the Tschuktchi.

The north-west of America had in Asia an especially good repute, for although it is rough and unfruitful in comparison with southern plains, and had not unjustly received the name of the American Siberia, yet it is not to be denied that in those parts where the new and the old world look so close in each other's faces, the former bears by far the mildest and most alluring aspect. The eastern extremities of Asia are lashed by the keen eastern tempests, and stand bleak, bare, without vegetation, the greater part of the year in ice and snow. The western shores of America, on the contrary, are protected from the east by high mountains. They are open to the mild westerly winds and ocean currents; they have a damper climate, and, in consequence, a more vigorous growth of trees and plants. In parts they are covered with fine forests down to the sea-shore. Here there is a contrast which is known to repeat itself in all northern countries. The ruder Sweden in the east contrasts in like manner with the milder Norway in the west; the desolate eastern coasts of Greenland buried in polar ice, with its western coasts inhabited and at times gay with verdure. Thus the great eastern country, the "Bolschaia Semla," rich in harbours, shelter, woods, and sea and land animals, might well, as I have said, become by report among the Asiatics "a Promised Land;" and this report may in the earliest times have played its tempting part in the first emigration of the primitive population of Asia to America.

All these attractive rumours circulated in Kamtschatka, in Okhotsk, Avatcha, and the other east-Asiatic ports founded by the Russians. They reached at last Moscow and Petersburg, and there found an attentive ear and a thinking head in which they fixed themselves. This head belonged to Peter the Great, who formed for himself the plan of reaching the great eastern land, America, from Siberia. The Czar Peter, who had himself either executed or prepared everything great that had been done in Russia, had shortly before his death drawn up instructions for his admiral, Count Apraxin, in which he enjoined him to take measures to have ships prepared in order with them to explore the coasts, and also to examine whether any of these were anyhow connected with the much-praised eastern land, or were separate from it.

It was then from this command of Peter the Great, first fulfilled by his successors and executrixes, Katherine I. and Elizabeth, that those renowned voyages and expeditions of discovery arose, which are known under the name of the "first" and "second Kamtschatkan expeditions," and which were both placed under the command of the distinguished Dane, Vitus Behring.

The first of these two expeditions of discovery set out from Petersburg under Katherine I. in the year 1725, and was finished in three years. They did not in this touch the shores of America, and yet they believed that they had nearly obtained the certainty that it was not a part of Asia. Captain Behring sailed along the coasts of Kamtschatka, the country of the Tschuktchi, so far to the north-east, till he observed, under 67° 18′ lat., that the coast curved round again to the west. From this he concluded that Asia was here surrounded by the sea.

Under the Empress Elizabeth, the daughter of Peter the Great, the foundress of the University of Moscow and the Academy of Fine Arts in Petersburg, that expedition which was called the "second Kamtschatkan," took place. This was one of the noblest, most fruitful in results, most brilliant enterprises of scientific discovery which had ever till then been executed, as well with regard to the aim which hovered before the adventurers, as also to the means and powers expended upon it.

By it, in the first place, was North-West America discovered; in the second place, the northern seas and islands of Japan were navigated and explored; in the third place, all Northern Asia was travelled over, accurately defined and described in a geographical point of view, and at length the question so long agitated by the English of the northern voyage round America back to Europe, solved. Several of the most distinguished Russian and German learned men and sailors, the already proved Behring, Spangberg, Tschirikow, the astronomers, naturalists, and historians, Gmelin, Steller, and others, were hereby called into play. Not only Germans, but also English, Swedes, and French. Delisle, Lesseps, Walton, Waxel, were employed. In regard, too, to the energy and endurance with which it was carried on and accomplished, this enterprise stood as yet completely alone, for it lasted sixteen years. Finally, as to the desired result, a number of the most valuable historical and scientific works have been produced by it, and the whole northern half of Asia, and a part of America, have for the first time been scientifically investigated and made known to the world.

All Siberia was, so to speak, flooded with men of science and their associates, as before with Cossacks, and the expedition was organised so as to embrace the whole region into a vast net. By tedious and toilsome processes the necessary means of subsistence, materials, and instruments were amassed at every station and central point. Along the rivers, along even the four thousand odd miles of coast on the icy sea, here and there were stationed magazines of supplies for the explorers and their attendants. From six to seven months were sometimes taken up in transporting the trees out of the forests to the ports in which the vessels were to be built for the voyage of discovery. Every one of these men of science had his region indicated to him in which he was to labour. Every captain had his river, which he was to reconnoitre, and his line of coast, which he was to explore. And almost at the same time small kindred expeditions sailed from all the rivers of Siberia and began at once their laborious work between ice and morass.

Each of them had assigned to him the mouth of a neighbouring river or a cape as the goal of his voyage, which he was to reach, sail round, and where he was to place himself in connexion with the other nearest expedition. Some of these exploring bands brought their mission to a speedy and successful end. Others were repeatedly beaten back, foundered, built new ships, and only after years of effort and adventure reached their goal — or perhaps never reached it at all.

I cannot here give details of the fate and the successes of each of these remarkable enterprises.

The voyage to the east, which principally concerns us here, was reserved by Captain Behring for himself. Captain Tschirikow accompanied him as second in command; and these two, with their ships St. Peter and St. Paul, sailed at last, on July 4, 1741, out of the Kamtschatkan harbour Avatcha, which was in consequence called St. Peter and St. Paul's Harbour, into the great eastern sea. And this same port has remained the chief harbour of preparation, or else the chosen place for rest and reparation for all the north-eastern voyages undertaken down to our time. Behring, like La Pérouse, Cook, and Kotzebue, put in here and collected his forces for arctic enterprise. This place, situated at the world's end, has indeed numerous monuments raised to Russian, French, English, and German circumnavigators of the world and discoverers, who there reached the termination of their toils.

To find the actual mainland of America, Behring and Tschirikow steered out of the Siberian waters south-eastwards into the vast Pacific, and cleft its waves where before them it had never yet been furrowed by keel of European ship.

They cruised about for months on this water waste, keeping on as much as possible towards the south-east, and their voyage was neither so brief nor so prosperous as the quiet westward voyage of Columbus towards the same land, whither the steady trade-winds had borne him, with sails always spread, within thirty days. Both ships became separated from each other in a storm, and they at length saw land at two different points, and somewhere about 57° lat., on the edge of that deep curve which the American coast forms there, southward from that colossal mountain which the Russians have named Mount Elias, and which, surpassing Mount Blanc many thousand feet in height, rises there a far-loooking watcher in the inner corner of this bay.

They observed that from this spot the shores of America inclined on one side to the south, and on the other turned back to the west to Siberia, whence they came. The two captains, separately, followed this coast to the west in their homeward voyage, touched it at various points, described their positions, discovered the chain of the Aleutian Isles, which on the outward voyage they had sailed past in tending too far to the south, and after half a year's voyage Tschirikow prosperously reached Kamtschatka and the haven of Peter and Paul.

Meanwhile commandant Behring and his partners in misfortune were tossed about and maltreated by storms, clouds, and snow-drifts. Sickness and death weakened and diminished their little company so sorely that at times there were not men enough in condition to set the sails and manage the rudder, and sometimes for days together the ship was driven hither and thither without steersman, a prey to the billows. At last, not far from Kamtschatka, they were wrecked on a desolate island, where Behring, after long illness, found a miserable death, and which was named from him "Behring's Isle." The rest of his party, after pining on this island a whole year in vain hopes of deliverance, constructed a bark from the fragments of their ship, ventured to sea in it, and at last reached the haven of Kamtschatka. They arrived, weakened by hunger and privations of all kinds, and in need of everything. In but one point they were well provided, namely, with the skins of a newly-discovered furry animal—the sea-beaver, as they called it—of which they had zealously pursued the chase on their island. The German naturalist Steller, the celebrated describer of Kamtschatka, who returned with this little band of sufferers, brought back for himself three hundred skins of this new animal, each of which would at that time be worth in the Chinese market one hundred dollars. This creature, whose delicate dark skin was the only thing that Behring's people saved from the shipwreck, has played in the history of the waters of the Northern Pacific, and in the discovery of North-Western America, too important a part not to deserve here an especial notice. The sea-beaver, or, as we now universally call it, the sea-otter (*Lutra marina*), inhabits exclusively the coasts of Kamtschatka, the Kourile, the Aleutian isles, and North America, as far down as California; in no other part of the world is it found. The fur is most handsome and costly in the northern regions; towards California it becomes of less value. It has probably long been known and prized by the Japanese, who from old times have had intercourse with the Kourile Islands. They and the inhabitants of Korea brought to the Chinese its beautiful fur, black as ebony, glossy, and streaked with silver hairs, which was sold for its weight in gold in Pekin.

But neither the Japanese nor the Chinese were aware of the extensive prevalence of this animal in the north; this was discovered, as we have mentioned, by the shipwrecked Russians under Behring. And when, in their intercourse with the Chinese, they made the second discovery, that the greatest profits could be drawn from the traffic in the skins of this animal, a desire seized them again to visit the coasts and islands of America, haunted by the sea-otter, and work out this new branch of trade. The sea-otter became for the conquest and colonisation of the Aleutian Isles and the north-west coasts of America, the same means of allurement, the same connecting link that the sable had been for that of Siberia. The chase of the sable had brought the Cossacks from the Ural to Okhotsk and to the Amoor. The chase of the sea-otter brought them thence by water one thousand versts further to the east, and to the new continent.

Just as a crowd of Cossacks and freebooters on horseback had hastened after Jermak on his crossing the Ural, so did similar freebooters in ships follow the Russian Columbus, Behring, on his opening the eastern ocean. On the part of the government no new expedition was so soon again undertaken. For some time following, all was done by private persons, merchants, hunters of sea-otters, and "Promischlennicks." It is to these latter that Russia is indebted for being endowed, or burdened, in addition to her steppes in Europe and frozen morasses in Asia, with that great desert of the North American peninsula, which is almost twice as large as Germany. From 1743, every year saw one or more expeditions accomplished, starting from Kamtschatka or Okhotsk, and ever penetrating further eastward from isle to isle, from promontory to promontory.

These undertakings were for the most part carried on by the speculating spirit and the capital of rich Russian merchants in Europe, from Moscow, Tula, Novogorod, &c. The poor inhabitants of the Aleutians were as much harassed and diminished in their number as the sea-otters.

From 1760 these trading voyages began to touch at the islands adjoining the American continent, the great island Kodiak, and the continent itself at the peninsula Alaska. A regular trading company was then established, organised like the great English trading companies, which undertook the whole business of otter-hunting, and other advantages to be derived from the Aleutian Isles and neighbouring lands, which they were further to explore and occupy.

The only Europeans settled on those shores of America which lie on the Pacific Ocean were then the Spaniards. They swayed these regions on a line of more than eight thousand miles from Cape Horn, in the south, northwards to California, and, according to their own claims, which they always supported with the old Papal bull of partition, further yet, " as far as these coasts extended to the north."

The discoveries of the Russians, and their steady advances towards the east and south, could not fail to excite the notice and solicitude of the Spaniards. The Spaniards had indeed under Cortez made some attempts to discover the north-west of America. But neither these attempts nor these expeditions under the viceroy Mendoza (the successor of Cortez) had brought them far beyond California. The rainy, stormy, mountainous, barbaric North-West appeared to them not very attractive, and they were the more willing to leave it in the unexplored obscurity which covered it, from the fear that the clearing up of this darkness might assist the English in finding out the long-sought north-west passage. But when all at once there appeared from quite another country wholly unexpected guests and rivals in the Pacific Ocean and in the north of America, the Spaniards waked out of their apathetic inactivity, and the viceroys of Mexico set themselves in motion to meet the Russians, and watch what they were about. From the year 1774, they sent out a series of expeditions towards the north-west, which sailed up the coast of America as far as the huge mountain Elias, the islands of Kodiak, and Unalashka, in order to look after the newly-arrived Russians. They touched at many points on the coast, and seized possession of them where they did not already find them occupied by the Russians. They pushed, too, their settlements, forts, and missions, further up towards the north, and at last took possession of those admirable ports of California, Monterey and San Francisco.

At the same time the English also set themselves in movement towards the north of the Pacific and the north-west of America. In the year 1776, they sent their great navigator Cook, who had already made two celebrated voyages in the South Pacific, on a third voyage, whose direction was round Cape Horn towards North America. Cook reconnoitred just those countries which till then the Spaniards and Russians had regarded as *their* exclusive province of discovery, and did it, too, in a more satisfactory and effective manner. His pioneering expedition was followed by a host of English trading enterprises. In the course of the decade 1780-90, many English captains sailed towards North-Western America, and threw themselves especially on those parts which lay central between the Russian possessions in the north and the Spanish in the south, lands in which the sea-otter skins were yet so abundant that the barbarous inhabitants used this costly fur for their ordinary mantles, bed-coverings, and tent-hangings. These articles, secured by the English traders, were brought over to China to adorn the proud mandarins of the Great Chan.

The French, too, sent at the same period their much-admired, much-lamented La Pérouse to the Pacific and the sea-otter coasts of North-Western America. A complete and general racing of the different nations now took place towards these, till then wholly neglected, parts of the earth. And in the next, as in the before-mentioned decennium, a host of private as well as government expeditions encountered each other, of Russians, Spaniards, English, and French, and at last of a people who, at the beginning of this race, took only a very late and very modest part, but who were destined in our century to compete with the Russians as arbiters in the North Pacific—namely, the North Americans from the Free States, or the "Boston men," as they were at that time called, after the state which fitted out the greater part of these expeditions.

It is not my design to enter here, where I treat of the progress of the Russians, into these voyages of other nations, and I have noticed them only to show how great a movement the Russian Cossacks set going in their capacity of first discoverers when they proceeded from the Ural Mountains, through Siberia, to America, and how the great work of the discovery of America was accomplished in the north-west, where it had so long stood still, if not by their sole act, yet by the impulsion they gave.

I may in passing, and at the conclusion, draw attention to the far-extending political consequences of that march led by the old equestrian chieftain Jermak three hundred years ago. Including her last acquisitions in Mantchooria, Russia now occupies in these districts, from the neighbourhood of Pekin to that of the gold regions lately discovered near Vancouver's Island, an extent of coast of more than four thousand geographical miles. No European or Asiatic power there holds sway over a like extent. And although statistics give us no great accounts of the wealth, culture, population, and political importance possessed by these regions, there is yet no foretelling of what development they may still be capable. There are to be found amongst them many favoured portions, such as the romantically beautiful country of Kamtschatka, with many a sheltered valley capable of cultivation; the navigable river Amoor, which equals the Danube in size; and of America the most favourable coast districts in such high latitudes. What surprises are before us in a nearer inspection of the mineral treasures of this reach of coast, after what we have experienced in the neighbourhood of Vancouver's Island, we cannot yet presume to determine. Russia holds, so to speak, in the grasp of her gigantic arms, the whole northern, half of the Pacific. She has become there the neighbour of England, of the United States, and of the Emperors of China and Japan; and, there, as elsewhere, she has become closely connected with the politics of the two former, and also concerned in the approaching changes and revolutions of the latter. It is not so long ago that Russia has pushed her colonies along the American coasts, already even down to the golden gates of San Francisco in California; that she has stretched a hand even into the centre of the Pacific, and was on the point of appropriating one of the Sandwich islands; and that she entertained the idea, which idea was moreover publicly announced in a ukase of the Emperor Alexander, of closing the whole Pacific north of the Sandwich Isles against foreign ships, and making it a "Russian lake," a "*mare clausum*" or, as it were, a Siberian sea.

But the freedom of the seas was ensured against these daring plans by an energetic and successful protest of all the powers. We seize, however, this occasion to remark how fain Russia is to recur to that testament of her Peter the Great, in which, as I said, an article on America and the Pacific Ocean is to be found.

CHAPTER V.

THE NORTH AND THE ENGLISH.

Martin Frobisher's Voyages to "Meta Incognita" (anno 1572-1578)—John Davis discovers Davis's Strait (1585)—Henry Hudson discovers Hudson's Bay (1610)—Bylot and Baffin discover Baffin's Bay (1616)—John Ross begins the Series of Arctic Expeditions of Modern Times (1818)—William Edward Parry penetrates into Lancaster Sound in the American Polar Sea (1816)—Sir John Franklin's Land Journey to the Coasts of the American Polar Sea (1820-21)—Sir John Franklin's last Voyage (1845)—M'Clure discovers the North-West Passage, and proves that America is surrounded by Water (Oct. 1850).

I HAVE already had opportunities of observing that, beginning with Columbus's first voyage, of all the great expeditions of discovery made by the enterprising European nations which have added to our knowledge of the new world, scarcely any have had this new world itself for their aim. As with Columbus and with the Portuguese, it was much rather the rich and populous Orient which they proposed for their goal. It was only by chance that they stumbled on America, and the first rejoicing at its discovery had no reference whatever to that country itself. It was India, the renowned of old, which they believed they had reached, and for which that rejoicing was meant.

To their annoyance the Europeans found the vast and barbarous barrier of America in their way, and circumstances almost forced them against their will to take notice of and explore it. It interested them much more to try to break through this barrier, or to avoid and sail round it somewhere or other.

By degrees it became known that the basin of the Atlantic, lying between the old world and the western continent, was a long and comparatively narrow valley. The only wide and convenient way out of this valley had from the first been taken possession of by the Portuguese. The passage round the Cape of Good Hope was called "the Portuguese Highway;" it might be called, too, the South-Eastern Passage. The second outlet through the southern end of America was found at length, as we have seen, by the Spaniards under Magellan. At that time it was called "the Spanish Highway;" and it might also be called the South-Western Passage. Thus, in the beginning of the sixteenth century, both the principal accesses to the much-coveted India were already in the possession of the southern, and, at that time, the chief maritime nations of Europe, and were partly blocked up by their stations and forts, or at least by their fleets. When, therefore, about the middle of that century, the northern nations likewise learned how to undertake long voyages, and, impelled by the longing for India, began to think of circumnavigating the globe, there remained nothing for them but either to make themselves masters of the Spanish or the Portuguese passage, or to find out a new one for themselves. Being too weak at first to think of conquest, they chose the latter alternative, and they cast their eyes in the first instance on the north-east of Europe.

The configuration of the lands and seas in that quarter was at that time almost unknown. Scarcely any conceptions about them existed but such as had been derived from Pliny, Strabo, and Ptolemy, whose works were constantly consulted about the north-east, just as they had formerly been cited by Columbus in respect to the west. As is now well known, these ancients had no conception of the great extension of Europe and Asia to the north and the east. They fancied the great ocean quite near, and reaching so far to the south that many of their geographers looked upon the Caspian Sea as a southern bay of the northern ocean. In consequence of such ideas, it was believed to be possible to sail round Asia in the north, and when once, in the time of the Emperor

Titus, as has been already related, a few Esquimaux were cast upon the shore of the North Sea, they were taken for natives of the East Indies whom storms had driven westward round the coasts of Asia and Europe.

On such false foundations in the sixteenth century did the geographical notions about the northern districts of Asia rest. It is true the Russians, who at that time had already crossed the long belt of mountains—the Ural—which separates Europe from Asia, and who had extended their rule, their hunting-grounds, and their fisheries to the shores of the Frozen Ocean, may have long had more correct ideas. But the Russians had not yet entered into the circle of civilized European nations, and had, as it were, to be discovered themselves by the latter. The English, who had studied Pliny, believed that the Asiatic continent ended in the north in a certain cape, called by the Romans Cape Tabin; and that if a voyage round this cape could once be accomplished, there would be found a sea way to China and India leading direct southwards. This Cape Tabin, therefore, became in the sixteenth century, so to say, the "Cape of Good Hope" for northern Asia.

These geographical notions, and the hopes built upon them, led to a whole series of so-called north-eastern voyages. The English were the first to try this way. In the beginning of the second half of the sixteenth century, their admiral, Sir Hugh Willoughby, and his companion, Richard Chancellor, sailed in this direction, provided, like Columbus on his voyage to the west, with passports and letters of introduction to the Great Khan and the Emperor of China. It will not surprise us with our present knowledge to learn that they were not able to deliver these letters, which stuck fast with their bearers in the icy bays to the north of Russia. However, these enterprises were not quite without result. If the English were unable to reach the Great Khan, they found at least Russia, made their appearance by way of Archangel before the Czar at Moscow, and laid the foundation of that commerce between Russia and England which has lasted to the present day. This discovery of Russia directed the thoughts of the English from their north-eastern passage to India; the most beneficial results of it being several journeys to Archangel, to Moscow, and, by way of the latter city, to the Caspian Sea.

Nevertheless, the possibility of circumnavigating the globe by a north-eastern track was by no means given up. Only another people took the enterprise in hand. It seems as if every seafaring nation had to go through the same circle of speculations, errors, and experiences. Towards the end of the century, the Dutch, seeing the English so much occupied with Russia, believed they could anticipate them in the north-east. At that time the energies of this people, like those of the English, had, in victorious conflicts with Spain, become developed, and their full-blown powers craved new occupations and enterprises. Learned men came forward, too, amongst them, who, following in the track of the old Greeks and Romans, converted one-half of Asia into water, and enterprising merchants gave willing credence to all they said. When, therefore, the Captains Cornelius Cornelsen and William Barenz, the first who were despatched to the north-east, discovered and sailed through the strait of Waygatz, reached a cape in the mouth of the river Ob, and then returned speedily with the joyful tidings that they had found Pliny's Cape Tabin, had even glanced round this point, and also received distinct information from the natives that the coast here extended directly to China, universal enthusiasm was kindled in Holland. A fleet of seven large vessels was soon fitted out, and the cities of Amsterdam, and Rotterdam, and others, as well as the Stadtholder, William of Orange, hastened to forward the undertaking. It is intelligible that this expedition, as likewise a third, did not gain the ends for which they were fitted out. At great cost of money and labour, nothing further was attained than the discovery of the desolate snow-clad coasts of Nova Zembla, and soon after the equally frozen rocks of Spitzbergen.

However, the Dutch, in seeking a way to India, found

at least shoals of whales and walruses, just as the English had found Russia and her products, and the Spaniards the Antilles, Mexico, and Peru. It is with nations as with individuals: we strive often after the high and dazzling aims that float before our fancy; we seldom reach them; but our earnest efforts find unlooked-for compensation on the way, and we are led aside to results and objects which at first we never contemplated.

Like as in England the far-famed mercantile Muscovite Company had been formed for the pursuit of Russian trade, in the same way in Holland the Greenland and Spitzbergen Company (Spitzbergen was then held to be a part of Greenland) arose from the capture of whales. The Dutch at last perceived that in the north good harpoons and fishing-tackle were better guides to wealth than all the letters of introduction from Prince William to the Emperor of China. They soon after founded, not far from the north pole, on one of the extremest capes of Spitzbergen, that remarkable settlement, Smeerenberg, where at the most flourishing period of the fishery about two hundred vessels and ten thousand men were collected, and forgetful of Cape Tobin, handed over to Russia the task of accomplishing the slow and toilsome discovery of the way to China and North Asia. This was found in the Overland Route described in the foregoing chapter.

The English meanwhile, with *their* views on India and China, had betaken themselves in another direction towards the north-west corner of the Atlantic Ocean, the only spot where it still appeared possible to emerge from this narrow basin. To this corner England was attracted more than any other country of Europe by her geographical position. The shape of her island, stretching far to the north-west, pointed like a magnet in that direction. "Our field is the north and north-west," exclaims an English author of that period, "the only field which the partition of the world has left to us." And when once this idea had taken fast hold of the nation, they devoted themselves to it with a patience and endurance which was really admirable. The long series of their enterprises for the discovery of the north-west passage has not its equal, if not in consideration of the results obtained, yet with regard to the energy, forethought and heroic spirit with which it was carried on. For three centuries have these English expeditions to the north-west been unweariedly pursued, with some few intervals, down to our days, forming, as it were, the fit crown and conclusion to the whole work of American discovery.

In order to understand the extraordinary tenacity of English belief in a non-existent passage, we must keep before our eyes, first, the important advantages promised by the discovery of such a route, and secondly, the prepossession which ancient representations as to the nature of the American continent had fostered in men's minds.

Half Siberia, as we have said, was ignored. The most northern districts of Asia were named India Superior (Upper India), although in reality nothing but Kamtschatka is to be found there. Japan was placed more to the north, and nearer to America, and therefore to Europe, than it is in fact. So they thought that from England to Japan and Upper India was but a single bound, and that bound once made, the highway of the Spaniards and Portuguese would be quite useless, and thus the treasures of the East would flow in from the north to England in far greater abundance. What was not to be hoped from such a passage! How earnestly must it not be sought!

The belief prevailed, too, that Nature had contrived the two great halves of America according to a certain harmonious plan. As she had made a channel (the Straits of Magellan) in the south, there must needs be a similar outlet in the north, and as if its existence had been fully made out, a name was given to it, that of the "Straits of Anian," derived from an old tradition. Also it was argued that the continent must come to a point in the north as it does in the south, and break up into islands. Another argument brought forward to establish the necessity of the case was that, else, the great breadth of America in the north would destroy the equilibrium of the globe.

It is true, soon after Columbus, the Cabots, the Cortereals, the Verazzani, and many other mariners whom I have already mentioned, had sailed along a large portion of North America, and had stumbled everywhere against mountains, capes, and frontiers of cliff. But had these men narrowly explored all the creeks, all the hiding-places and mysterious recesses there? As far as their own practical and cursory reconnoitring went, might not the whole be just as well a large complex of islands as the connected mass of a continent? From Florida to the ice-fields of Baffin's Bay there is not a branch of the sea, not a creek, on which the hope of a north-west passage had not been hung in turn, not the mouth of a river or bay into which some navigator had not sailed, in the expectation of opening a communication with the west. Nor is there a mountain in the interior of the land, from the Alleghanies to the Rocky Mountains, which some pioneer wandering towards the west has not climbed with the idea that the prospect of the South Sea would present itself to him at the top, as once to Balboa from the mountains of the Isthmus of Panama.

Not only do we easily believe what we wish, but in all ages there have been found inventive minds who make it their business to flatter our wishes with delusive phantoms. And it was the effort to gratify the ruling desire of northern Europe that gave birth to many fabulous tales of voyagers who had actually gone round North America and sailed out from the Pacific Ocean into the Atlantic. This was first asserted of a Portuguese, Martin Chaque, who, in a voyage from India to Portugal, about the middle of the sixteenth century, was said to have been driven on the Pacific towards the north; then, continually sailing north-east, to have run by many islands, and at last to have come out into the Atlantic Ocean off Newfoundland.

In the same manner the report sprang up in Ireland that some years after this Chaque, a certain Andreas Urdaniata had really found a passage across in the year 1557. He had, it was related, sailed out of the Pacific Ocean, right through America to Europe, and had carried the information to the King of Portugal. The latter, however, it was said, had strictly enjoined on him silence about his adventure, lest when the English heard of it they should prove seriously annoying both to him and the King of Spain.

But of all the untrustworthy accounts of voyages of this kind, the one that made the greatest noise in the world, and was most universally accepted, was that of the far-famed Greek, Juan de Fuca. De Fuca had been long a seaman in the Spanish service, and in that capacity made many voyages in the east and west seas. He offered to an English diplomatist, whom he came across at Venice, to enter Queen Elizabeth's service, and show the English the "Straits of Anian" (the northern Straits of Magellan) and the north-west passage through America to Cathay (China). He had, he said, discovered it on a mission from the viceroy of Mexico. Under 47° of latitude the continent of America, by his account, curved at California to the east, in a wide opening in which he had sailed right on for twenty days. Then the water expanded again, and he perceived at once that he was in the North Sea, and had found the entrance into the Atlantic Ocean. Upon this discovery he had speedily turned back into the Pacific Ocean, returned to Mexico, and made his report to the viceroy, but neither from him nor from the King of Spain had he received the reward he expected for so great a discovery. The Englishman to whom De Fuca imparted this could not at first make him any offer in the name of his government. When, afterwards, this was practicable, and they sought De Fuca, they found he had died in the mean while.

Similar legendary tales of voyages, rumours, traditions, myths, have sprung up at divers times like *ignes fatui*, and appeared to the north-west explorers like guiding stars. They all had this in common, that they were related and accepted as true amongst the English, the Dutch, and especially in the north of Europe, but that they were first borrowed from the southern nations, the Spanish and Portuguese. The North desired to find the north-west passage, the South desired that it should not be found. The Spaniards and Portuguese had gone to work so secretly with their discoveries, their colonies, and their charts, that they were popularly held to be omniscient, and it was maintained that they had long known the north-west passage, and had passed backwards and forwards through America, carefully letting no one find out where this passage lay.

In the year 1572 Queen Elizabeth despatched for that purpose Martin Frobisher, who undertook three voyages to the north-west of America, discovered several islands, sailed through a narrow channel, which was named after him, "Frobisher's Straits," and several more passages, which he firmly believed to lead to Cathay. Queen Elizabeth gave to this remote land the mystical name of "*Meta Incognita*" (the unknown goal), and this Meta Incognita, this Cape of Good Hope of North America, long played there the same part and deceived men with the same vain hopes as in the north-east the beforementioned "Cape Tabin." Elizabeth wished to build a fort there to secure to herself the route thence to India, in the same manner as the Spaniards had secured the south-west passage through the Straits of Magellan. She wished likewise to have gold mines worked there, her trusty Admiral Frobisher having brought back with him small quantities of a certain bright yellow stone which the London goldsmiths in their blindness pronounced to contain gold. On his third voyage, in the year 1578, Frobisher arrived there with no fewer than fifteen vessels. All, however, ended in smoke, the gold-dust, of which they had carried whole ship-loads to England, being at last recognized as a very common kind of earth. The fortress and settlement perished in ice and snow, the ships were dispersed, and the geographical discoveries of Frobisher were so uncertain, and wrapped by himself in such mystery, that it has long since continued to be a question where, in fact, he got sight of the north, what land was Queen Elizabeth's Meta Incognita, and what might be the channel called Frobisher's Straits.

Nevertheless, it is said that Queen Elizabeth was "well satisfied" with her brave knight Frobisher, and the result of his voyages. She believed that he had clearly proved the possibility of a passage to China. The English merchants were of the same opinion, and soon after Frobisher's death similar expeditions were got up, both by government orders and at the expense of private individuals. George Weymouth, John Davis, Henry

Hudson, Thomas Button, Baffin, were the names of the men who, at the end of the sixteenth, and at the beginning of the seventeenth century, with China and India in their heads, and new letters of introduction to the Great Chan in their pockets, ran one after the other, from Bristol, Plymouth, Falmouth, and other small harbours of Western England, and directed their course north-west, to reach and to sail round the "unknown goal," and so "to get to the rear of the Spaniards and Portuguese in the Pacific Ocean." Almost every one of these believed that he had really found the straits which led thither, or, at least, had seen them from a distance, and almost every one then, without having completed the passage itself, returned home speedily with this joyful news. The hope was kept alive especially by the information of Davis, who, in 1585, passed through the wide straits named after him Davis's Straits, and found, everywhere to the north and north-west, sea, full of ice it is true, but still sea. And when the great navigator Hudson, who made in the regions of the north more numerous and important discoveries than any of his predecessors, had opened the other great straits and the wide inland sea which yet bears his name, the whole mystery was at last supposed to be solved. They regarded Hudson's Straits as those very Straits of Anian so long and so vainly sought for, which linked together the Atlantic and Pacific Oceans, and Hudson's Bay itself, as a part of this western sea.

All eyes and all expectations were now, of course, directed to Hudson's Bay, in which, like his predecessor, the Portuguese Cortereal, Hudson himself had perished. Many of his countrymen followed him, and another northern nation, the Danes, took part in these Hudson's Bay expeditions. Denmark was just at that time ruled by a king who knew how to stimulate the development to the national power, as Fancis I. in France, and Elizabeth in England, had done. This king was her much-lauded Christiern IV. He, like James I., sent a series of navigators to Davis's and Hudson's Straits, to Greenland, to Anian's Straits, and the "unknown goal." But the only result, which in the end all these English and Danish voyagers to their vexation obtained, was the knowledge that Hudson's Bay was again blocked up by land, that none of its inlets and creeks led to the west, but rather that it represented a large basin or gulf, like the Gulf of Mexico.

Meanwhile, on this occasion, every corner of that sea was explored and thoroughly made known, and, if neither in England nor Denmark these experiences were thought sufficient to found upon them a South Sea Company, at least in Denmark a "New Greenland," and in England the far-famed "Hudson's Bay Company" were established, the latter growing at last out of that lately discovered inland sea into the sovereign of all North America, and appropriating a more extensive territory than perhaps in any period of history was ever possessed by a trading company.

After all the hopes that had been built on Hudson's Bay being a direct road to the west, the confident assertions that it had a western outlet, the large sums that the Danish and English kings had spent upon it, the sight of rocks, glaciers, woods, and morasses on all sides presenting an impassable barrier to all further advance, might well, as it did, fill with despair the adherents of the north-west passage, and cause the whole idea for a long time to be put aside.

To this were added the internal disquiet and revolutions of England in the middle of the seventeenth century. It is true, these drove many Britons forth upon the ocean; but these were poor persecuted people, who sought a new fertile country in America where they might exist in peace. The waste lands of the north could not allure them, nor did they at all feel themselves called to the business of geographical discovery, or to the difficult accomplishment of a passage to China. Cromwell, indeed, did much towards the development of England's naval power. But his only object was to strengthen the warlike part of it, in order to intimidate hostile neighbours. He no more cared for geographical discoveries than those emigrant "Pilgrim Fathers."

The erection of the Hudson's Bay Company was, or became, a third hindrance to the progress of Northwestern exploration, an obstacle that began in 1669, and operated for a long while unfavourably. The privileges of this company were very extensive. They were to possess for their own all the coasts and regions round Hudson's Bay, and alone enjoy the right of trading and fishing there. Thus did all those northern seas and lands come into the hands of this company, who found it accord with their interests to close the bay, to refuse entrance to all curious or invidious comers, and, as the Spaniards had done with the South Sea, to make it a *mare clausum*. They erected several forts on the shores of Hudson's Bay, despatched thither every year, at fixed periods, vessels which brought English wares, and returned with the rich furs which their governors and agents had obtained from the American Indians. They did not trouble themselves about geographical discoveries, and tried for a long time to hinder them. They were, in truth, as much afraid as the Spaniards of the discovery of a north-west passage. Such a discovery, they thought, might turn the whole stream of commerce and the voyages of private speculators that way, and all their privileges and fur monopoly would then come to an end. They were, in fact, accused of having, by corruption, beguiled into false and unfavourable statements the captains of the exploring ships which once, in the beginning of the eighteenth century, the English Government did send for the investigation of certain not well-known recesses of Hudson's Bay. These highly privileged fur-traders kept extremely close the geographical information which they had obtained concerning North America, and the charts and memoirs of their archives, and, in a word, endeavoured to veil in clouds from the great public the whole region that they had explored, and to keep it, as it were, completely under lock and key.

Hudson's Bay appeared no longer to offer an opening anywhere, and with regard to the great gulf named after Baffin, the extremely laconic reports of that old illustrious navigator were considered sufficient—to the effect that this, like the Gulf of Mexico and Hudson's Bay, was completely surrounded with land and mountains.

There is another direction, too, which I have not as yet touched upon, but which can only be regarded as a branch of the north-west voyages in which the gates of discovery appeared for a long while to stand open, namely, directly across the north pole between Greenland and Spitzbergen; and simultaneously with the already described north-west voyages took place a series of attempts which may be called POLAR VOYAGES, or voyages for the discovery of a NORTHERN PASSAGE.

About the middle of the sixteenth century, at an epoch, therefore, when no one had ventured far beyond the European "North Cape," the above-mentioned parts of the globe were believed to be formed as follows. Just at the north pole it was supposed there stood a black colossal rock which lifted its lofty head to the fixed Polar star. Around this polar rock, they asserted, flowed an open sea, and this sea was encircled in all the quarters of the compass by four islands of equal size. Four colossal straits or currents proceeding from the great ocean divided these islands, and through these channels the superfluous waters of the ocean flowed away, collected themselves in the basin that surrounded the pole, and, dashing loudly round the "polar rock," plunged into the innermost abysses and bowels of the earth. The legend added, that these four large islands were very fruitful, and had the finest and healthiest of climates ("*insulæ optimæ et saluberrimæ*"), and that those nearest to the Atlantic ocean were inhabited by a race of pigmies.

This traditional picture of the polar regions is, to be found amongst others in the works and maps of the cosmographers of the Emperor Charles V. When the English and Dutch, at the end of the sixteenth century, began their voyages towards the north-east, towards Norway and Russia, and when they gradually discovered the outlines of Nova Zembla, Spitzbergen, and Greenland rising out of the ocean, they found the sea around the pole for the most part barricaded by an impenetrable belt of icebergs and fields of ice. But those old ideas of a fair and friendly "isle of pigmies" at the frozen pole, and the picture, so natural to men under all circumstances, that beyond their misty horizon lay something far more beautiful—a very ancient Greek legend had, indeed, already placed this land of the happy and ever-healthy hyperboreans, this earthly paradise, high up towards the north pole—these representations, I say, induced the belief that at the north pole would be found again open sea, quiet and navigable waters, and a mild climate, if only it were possible to pierce through the terrible barriers of ice off Greenland and Spitzbergen. Many mariners affirmed, from their own observation, that the climate became again to the north better and quite warm; north of Spitzbergen the sun had melted the tar from the ships' planks. Nay, poetry and illusion here, too, lent their aid to the excited imagination, and here, as in the north-west expeditions, reports of polar voyages actually executed were popularly current. Several Dutchmen boasted that they had penetrated to the north pole; and one of them said that he had twice sailed round the north pole with the polar star right over his head, under the brightest sunshine, on water smooth as a mirror, and with sails swelled by most favourable gales.

All this led to the conjecture that it was possible to arrive at the Pacific ocean and China, if not by the northeast passage along the shores of Asia, nor even by the north-west route through America, yet by a northern passage between Greenland and Spitzbergen. This idea was all the more eagerly entertained, that this direct northern route is of course the straightest line that can be drawn between China and England, and the shortest of all the ocean ways. Already in the beginning of the sixteenth century, under the protectorate of the still flourishing "Muscovite Company," which devoted so much attention to all particulars relating to the north, had a series of expeditions been fitted out, to pursue this direction. The great sea hero, Hudson, had himself led one of these early polar expeditions, and other navigators followed in his wake. But all either remained stuck in the blocks of ice encircling the pole, or they were driven aside from their original purpose by the profitable and alluring whale fishery which met them on the way, and thus degenerated from adventurous discoverers to mere fishers for whale-oil and seal-blubber. The voyage of a certain Captain Fotherby in the seventeenth century was the last of this first series of polar voyages. After him for a time men contented themselves with the whale fishery, left the pole alone, and went no further than the pursuit of these living lumps of fat led them.

Taken altogether, this state of things lasted through the eighteenth century, though even this period was not without various continually renewed attempts. But these attempts led scarcely to any new discoveries; for even the great Cook, when he sailed through Behring's Straits, could only attain to a northern *non plus ultrà* which we in these days should describe as a tolerably southern region. The English may have prosecuted these discoveries in the ice and darkness of the pole less energetically because they had in the mean while found the other route to India through the light and fire of the tropics. By sailing round Africa they had taken possession of India, as the Portuguese had formerly done, and had enough to do to organise their southern watertracks and acquisitions. Then came the continental war, which arose out of the French revolution, and gave a blow to all the peaceful and scientific undertakings of England.

But soon after the peace of Paris began that unparalleled succession of voyages to Arctic America, which, pursued during a full half-century, have at last ended in our days with the result that the furthest extremities of the American continent have been unveiled, the north-west passage explored, and the new world for the first time entirely sailed round on salt water, and laid before our eyes as an island.

The first of these astonishing voyages was made by Captain John Ross, in 1818. This "Nestor of the modern arctic heroes," as the English name him, had the commission to pierce through Baffin's Bay into the realm of Boreas, and force his way by Behring's Straits out into the South Sea. On the fulfilment of such a voyage the English Parliament had set a reward of 20,000*l.*; on the attainment of at least half the way, a lesser prize of 5000*l.* But Ross reached neither the one nor the other goal. He went all round Baffin's Bay, and returned home with the tidings that old Baffin had been quite right; the whole of Baffin's Bay was, in fact, as he had represented it, a land-locked basin of water. Even in the background of the so-called Lancaster Sound, said Ross, he had plainly seen land and mountains too, and this, likewise, was nothing but a gulf.

But on this latter important point William Edward Parry, commander under old Ross, was not of the same opinion as his chief. Strong objections were raised by this young, bold, sharp-sighted man against the existence of the "mountains" and "backgrounds" of Lancaster Sound. No one had set foot on these mountains, not even a boat had ever approached them. Perhaps they were only floating icebergs, or even mere clouds. To subject this point to investigation, Parry set out next year with two ships. He soon arrived at the mouth of Lancaster Sound, and sailed up it, first in strained and anxious expectation, but soon in triumph. The mountains of old Ross had disappeared, the sea was open and free, and a long, wide channel showed itself, which Parry called "Barrow's Straits." Through the ice-fields which he met here and there he forced, sawed, bored his way with his ships, and so advanced three hundred German miles far westward into the Northern Ocean, into an archipelago of large islands, which no mortal eyes from Europe had seen before him, and which were rightly named, after him, "Parry's Isles." He had already overstepped the western line, for the attainment of which the British Parliament had offered a reward of 5000*l.*; already had he announced to his crew that now the other "20,000*l.* line" would be reached; already he believed Behring's Straits near, and thought they *must* succeed in sailing over into the waters of Eastern Asia. Already, I say, Parry believed himself to have touched the goal, when at the farthest capes of the large "Melville Island," at the end of the long straits he had sailed through, a sea full of icebergs and storms appeared before him. During his efforts to pierce through it, the brief hours of the arctic summer fleeted away, and as early as August the northern winter stretched forth its grim arms and took the bold adventurer and his comrades prisoners. They wintered twelve hundred miles from the north pole, in deep ice and snow, and in a five-months night, occupied with astronomical and other observations, with geographical and naturo-historical excursions, in a waste where for hundreds of miles all around them there was not a sentient being, and whither, in spite of all the exertions of thirty long years after, no one has succeeded in penetrating again. Never yet had an incursion into the arctic chaos that pierced so far and so prosperously been executed.

Contemporaneously with Parry's voyage the English government had given orders for an expedition by land, which was designed to penetrate the territories of the Hudson's Bay Company towards the north, in order, if possible, to hold out somewhere a helping hand to Parry, and which was placed under the command of the noble Sir John Franklin.

Franklin reached with indescribable toil the extreme end of the mainland—which before him had merely been seen from two points in the far distance, by two celebrated travellers of the fur company, Mackenzie and Hearne—wintered in its neighbourhood, travelled over it, discovered and explored a stretch of coast upwards of eight hundred miles long, but sought in vain for Parry, who, as I said, had in the mean while stuck fast in the ice one thousand miles north of him. The disasters and privations which Franklin, his scientific friends Dr. Richardson and Hood, and their other admirable companions underwent on this journey can scarcely be described in a small compass. They wandered about for months in open boats, on those inhospitable shores, struggling with storms, breakers, masses of ice, and hostile Esquimaux. When the usual preserved food of travellers in those regions, the "pemmican," as it is called (buffalo flesh, dried, scraped, and packed in leathern sacks), was come to an end, they were compelled to support themselves with difficulty on the berries and mosses which grow scantily on the rocks of the north coast. For festivals and holidays they had to wring their repasts from bears and wolves, and whatever skin and bone these savage beasts left behind them they carefully collected, dried, and pulverised between stones, and prepared their soup from such refuse. When not a bone more was to be found under the snow, they felt their own meagre bodies, and examined their clothing, to discover if yet a piece of leather or a strap remained to stew. Partly forsaken by their people, whom famine and cold were decimating, threatened by some mutinous spirits with conspiracy and murder, the little suffering band—the martyrs of science—crept over the unknown region of ice in the direction of home, constantly, even in the midst of the greatest distress, keeping their scientific aims before their eyes. Even when their fever-shaken skeleton forms were already under the hand of death, they made their astronomical, meteorological and magnetic observations, and with their trembling, frostbitten, emaciated fingers, put them to paper. If then, in order to relieve their feeble shoulders, they at last threw almost everything aside, they still preserved their journals and reports for the government and the nation. They could at last scarcely, with their changed and ghastly voices, which sounded as if coming out of the grave, make communications to each other, or exhort each other mutually to ENDURANCE, COURAGE, and HOPE. A couple of friendly Indians, heaven-sent messengers, who at last came one day among these few despairing sufferers with some just-shot venison, saved and preserved for us Franklin, who was to give the world so many more disclosures still as to a part of our globe never before visited, and who, undismayed by the want and anguish already endured—like Schiller's diver—a second and a third time plunged into the cold gloom of the north to fill the goblet of science.

Parry, too, returned again more than once and completed his earlier discoveries. Old Ross also returned once thither, convinced himself of the navigableness of Lancaster Sound—that arctic Gibraltar which he once fancied closed—and planted the British flag on the spot discovered by him, which is the central point and pole of all the magnetic forces vibrating in the heart of the terrestrial globe. And when finally the noble Franklin, in the year 1845, entered for the third time into that El Dorado of natural wonders and the most exciting sea-adventures, and there—with one of the most splendid outfits which England ever supplied, and with a picked company of officers and sailors, and young amateurs of arctic sports—disappeared from sight, and when the Secretary of the Admiralty had said that this expedition of Franklin's should be the last despatched by England for the circumnavigation of America, this prophecy was so far from being fulfilled, that it actually was the cause of the north swarming with fleets.

In the year 1847, Franklin's expedition was expected to return. On its non-arrival that year anxiety arose, and when in the next it still remained away, the anxious wife and troubled friends of the missing hero stirred up the government, and the whole British nation, to use the most vigorous measures for his rescue. A searching expedition went out in 1848, under the command of the experienced south and north pole navigator, the younger Ross, to Baffin's Bay, and a second went forth to sail round the world to Behring's Straits, in order to watch and work at the two outlets of the great polar basin. These two searching expeditions were followed, in 1849 and 1850, by a succession of others. The Hudson's Bay Company, too, ordered a journey by land through the deserts belonging to them, under the charge of the scientific inquirer, Dr. Richardson, the faithful friend and former companion in suffering of Franklin. The American merchants took the warmest share in this benevolent chase, and one of them, Mr. Grinell, presented the government with a sum of money which served to fit out two vessels.

The whole civilised world looked on these noble and remarkable exertions of the Anglo-Saxon people for the recovery of their countrymen and friends with the greatest sympathy and earnest expectation. Although several earlier scientific expeditions—for instance that of La Pérouse—had disappeared similarly, and been sought for with similar zeal, yet anything to equal this had never yet been experienced.

For three hundred years the north-west passage had been the cherished idea, the object of constant pursuit to the British. Many of the dearest memories of their naval service were associated with it; their most distinguished navigators had either taken part in or been formed by it; and now the most beloved of all, on whom more than on any other had the world placed its hopes that he would set the crown on the work, had vanished—together with all his brave comrades—without a trace.

Sir John Franklin, the gentle and spirited discoverer of the north coast of America,—with whose great sufferings in behalf of science and the great national object the whole nation was acquainted, and which had called forth the sympathy of the whole reading public of Europe,—a man whom neither the cannibals nor the hideous aspect of a death by starvation had deterred,—and moreover a man of whom the Indians themselves related with wonder that he had not the will to hurt a fly, that he drove the mosquitoes out of the tent with only a fly-flap, without doing them any harm, or had merely blown away these bloodsuckers from the hand that held the pen,—such a man, I say, who was perhaps even then—as once before—on the Sea of Bears, living on moss, shaken by fever, a half-starved skeleton, suffering in silence, and encouraging his faithful little band by his example, still wandering about on some concealed icy shore,—such a man was worth saving! His despairing widow, and the many mourning families of the other hundred and fifty brave officers and crew, were worth consoling. A wonderful emulation was suddenly kindled. In the course of the last ten years no fewer than thirty-five well-fitted out ships, with more than one thousand zealous and experienced seamen have one after another gone forth. Behring's Straits, Baffin's Bay, Lancaster Sound, Barrow's Straits, and other branches were beset with watchers. In every opening, in every frozen portal, in every recess, where one could cherish the least hope of the discovery, did these searching expeditions labour in an indescribable conflict with the savage powers of Nature, and the regions of the north pole were thus more full of life than they had ever been.

The most extraordinary means, the most unusual telegraphs were contrived in order to convey tidings and signals to their countrymen, still perhaps breathing somewhere. The ships sent up here and there little balloons with letters fastened to them, in the hope that the wind might blow them far off, and bring them to Franklin. They forged copper collars, and engraved on them news for Franklin; then they caught wolves, foxes, birds, and other creatures, fixed the collars round their necks, and let them loose again, in the hope that Sir John might shoot one of these animals, and make use of the signals thus conveyed. They put aside all that could possibly be spared of the provisions, packed dried meat, and other food that would keep a long while in bags and chests, buried and walled them up here and there on the coast, and then wrote on the rocks: "There, under that block, north-east from this rock, two hundred steps from the sea-beach, lies food for Sir John Franklin and his comrades!"

In every Esquimaux hut, too, they deposited a similar

writing, and commissioned these migrating people to spread the tidings everywhere they could in those ice-labyrinths and snow-wastes. Wherever a projecting headland or conspicuous crag was to be found, they painted it white and wrote in great red letters a similar greeting to Sir John Franklin.

In this manner they filled the whole northern archipelago with guide-posts, letters, questions, and sighs. And when they found him nowhere, they finally concluded that he had broken through the polar circle of ice and rocks to the "*Polynia*"—the free and open sea round the pole, of which the old fables began to be revived. There, thought they, he was perhaps wandering like a swan frozen up in a tank, round and round the dark pole, seeking in vain for an outlet to the brighter south.

That this representation was false, as was probably the whole idea of the ocean-pool encircling the pole we first learned a short while ago, since it became a certainty that Franklin found his death, not as a triumphant discoverer of the north pole, but as one defeated and already on his return to England. His grave, or the last traces of him, have been found and recognised in a tolerably southern latitude, in the territory around the mouth of the great Fish River.

Parry and Franklin—these were the two chief names in the history of the discovery of the north of America. These were the two men who carried out there the most decisive actions. The one disclosed the arctic Pillars of Hercules, Lancaster Sound, and Barrow Straits, through which alone it is possible to penetrate with ships into the northern labyrinth. The other was the first to unfold the northern continental coast of America. Lyons, Rae, Belcher, Beechey, Keene, and all the others who followed them, have only built upon the foundations already laid, traced further the northern shores sketched by Franklin, and pointed out the various branches of the great channel first disclosed by Parry. Nevertheless, each one of these men brought back with him one or two stones wherewith to build up the edifice of North American discovery—one a new peninsula, another an island, the third a stretch of coast, the fourth an ocean-strait or a great river; and moreover they brought with them their excellent journals published over all the world, which are rich to overflowing in the most interesting observations and speculations on climate, natural history, and ethnography. And thus, from all these fragments and scattered links of the chain, we are able to put together the whole picture of the north as it has existed unobserved since the beginning of the world, and been able to follow to its remotest boundaries the whole terrestrial life which there seems to vibrate in low and faint pulsations.

Our zoologists now know the most remote haunts of the cetacea and fishes which animate the polar seas. They no longer ask whither in summer the birds of passage fly, they have found out their nests, which they build there on the smooth ice, and from which they swarm forth to the south. They know how far the reindeer, the elk, the remarkable cloven-footed creatures, yet clad in fur, like the bear—the musk oxen—which may well be called the "horned cattle of the north pole," pursue their excursions, and how far they can find pasture. They have seen the last traces which the polar bear prints on the snow, and heard the furthest howl of the wolf die away in the noiseless air of the pole. The botanist has inspected all the stages of vegetation, from the lofty pines of Canada downwards to the scanty dwarf willow-bushes, which straggle here and there on the North American coasts and on its "barren grounds" —as on the edges of the Alpine glacier—down to the yet lowlier grasses and mosses which lend in spring a streak of greenness even to "Parry's Island;" down to the microscopic little fungi which in the "Arctic Highlands" here and there at least tinge the snow with red.

Nor have the ethnographer and the historian gone out from these admirable voyages of discovery with empty hands. For so complete has been the investigation of one of the most remarkable races on the earth, that we now know scarcely any people in the world so fully as the Esquimaux. We now overlook almost all the far extending localities of these races who have attached themselves to the northern coasts for a length of so many hundred miles, and scattered their children as far as the whale, the seal, the moose, and the musk-ox wander. These poor Esquimaux, whom our ancestors abhorred as devil-worshippers ("everywhere here the devil is worshipped," is written in large letters on a mediæval map of North America, and in the reports of the first discoverers of the Esquimaux land we may read that the English sailors sometimes compelled these people to pull off their boots in order to see if they had not cloven-feet like the Evil One), these calumniated Esquimaux, I say, are now better known. We have seen that there are in their ice-huts thinking beings, even poets and philosophers, that even there the glorious spark which God kindled in the breast of the first man glimmers still, and at times breaks forth in a bright flame, that even there, on the everlasting snow-fields, a sprightly human race is swarming and stirring, and that wit and frolic gush forth in the time of youth (read Parry's description of Esquimaux boys) even at the north pole.

Parry, Franklin, and many more of the men who led these arctic expeditions, were characters not only so persevering, bold, and energetic, but also so benevolent, gentle-hearted, scientifically educated, and at the same time guarded against all external temptations, as only the humanised Christian modern times have produced. In their natures were coupled a solid moral strength and manly firmness, with the tenderest susceptibility of feeling,— a beautiful union most frequently found in the noble and masculine British race.

They were in a much higher degree fitted for the arduous work of exploration amongst savage countries and peoples than any of their predecessors. The arts and sciences which they found in existence furnished them with an abundance of means and apparatus to use on their way which could never before have been supplied to an investigating discoverer. Their ships and boats were constructed on a system invented especially for the north, and prepared for the rough handling which they would receive from the icebergs and floes. Their scientific preparations were most brilliant, and if we look over the list of the instruments sent with them, the newly-invented appliances for the minutest measurement of time or the manifold properties of air and water, for the investigation of the sea in all its depths, for the definition of electric and magnetic forces, one is tempted to say that what were sent out to the north pole were not ships, but floating observatories and mathematical astronomical cabinets. Even the petty arts and artificers of common life were called on to serve after their fashion. They contrived the most suitable clothes to bestow on the northern voyagers, and chemists and cooks invented the most trustworthy methods of packing and preserving the provisions, till they brought it to the point of making flesh, milk, and eggs capable of keeping fresh for years, and thus the discoverers were enabled to maintain life through several winters, far from all the slaughter-houses, vegetable-markets, and poultry-yards of the old world.

The officers were chosen from among the best and most educated men, and even in the common sailors—as if the cause were indeed a holy one—moral qualities were more carefully sought for than would usually be the case in recruiting for the convent and the monastic orders. Only such as were of blameless morals were accredited with the courage and endurance which were so necessary for the attainment of the difficult goal. The followers of Columbus, without zeal for discovery, tried to throw him overboard; Hudson was murdered by his; and a like fate befel many other renowned adventurers of the early time at the hands of their rebellious crews, who could not enter into the great plans of their leaders, and who were impatient of the exertions demanded from them. No such case has ever occurred in the modern British north-west expeditions, and the annals of these form in this respect a spotless page of history on which the philanthropist's glance is fain to linger.

The scurvy, that dreaded pest of seamen, had often swept away whole crews, and caused the finest enterprises to founder. But now such wise measures were taken against the enemy, that sometimes these expeditions did not lose a single man. All the anti-scorbutic plants had been carefully studied, and well-filled medicine chests provided. The commanders even built close to the stoves in their cabins little hot-houses, in which they cultivated the plants which were beneficial against scurvy. These plants, deprived of light through the long polar nights, grew up colourless and white, but kept, nevertheless, all their wonted healing qualities.

For the relief of tedium and inactivity (the foundation of so much evil), which lead naturally to discord and sickness of soul and body, care was taken. Musicians were taken on board, and collections of instructive and entertaining works provided. In the melancholy winter-quarters of the north, where the snow lay piled mountain-high round the vessels and made all exit impossible, they set going games on the ice. The officers instituted schools on board, and daily instructed their men. They published journals, under an officer's editorship, in which every one put down his ideas. Masked balls were set up, and stages erected, on which the mimetic talent was exercised, the commanders of the vessels themselves writing appropriate plays. Thus many a one returned from those gloomy snow wastes to England, whence he had departed a mere ignorant seaman, not only better and more patient, but also more skilful and more instructed.

The English have expended almost as much time and toil on the scientific conquest of this their northern ice-labyrinth, as on the subjugation of the golden realms of India. These two acquisitions are both to be ranked among their greatest and most splendid national undertakings. In a comparison of the results to which they attained in each, one can scarce refrain from a smile while contrasting the populous Bengal and all its rich abundance with Boothia, the haunt of three hundred poor seal-fishers; Melville Island, inhabited by polar bears, with the sunny Ceylon so rich in all forms of creation; the world-famous Calcutta, Delhi, and Benares of Hindostan, with the obscure "Iglooliks" and "Unumacks" of the Esquimaux; when we see how there one populous principality after another was annexed, often with but little show, and here with what triumph the discovery of the melancholy Bathurst's Island, or the stormy passage through Regent's Inlet was greeted! "Victoria Land," "King George's Sound," "Coronation Gulf," what splendid names were invented, what comfortless solitudes were honoured with them, and yet thought worthy of an almost more detailed and graphic description than was given to many an Asiatic kingdom.

The comparison might, as I have said, provoke a smile. Yet how pleasant are not the observer's feelings if he then compares the manner in which these strangely contrasted conquests were achieved, and draws a parallel between the actors in the two scenes! Here all was transacted in kindness and friendship with the natives, who there were reduced to a servile condition. Indeed, the British ships which appeared on those frozen shores were for the period of their stay places of refuge, hospitals, and poor-houses for the suffering humanity there, for the poor native Esquimaux, in which the hungry were fed, the sick ministered to, and the naked clothed.

Among the many efforts, enterprises, and labours, which brought all this to pass, and which I regret not to be able to paint here in detail, I must, in conclusion, place only one fact and one remarkable point of time in a somewhat clearer light. I mean the interesting incidents and circumstances in consequence of which it was finally made out that America was completely surrounded by salt water, and that the long-sought "north-west passage" really existed.

Among the various search expeditions which were despatched in quest of Franklin, was one which, in 1850, under the command of Captain Collinson, was sent to Behring's Straits in order thence to work its way eastwards. Captain Collinson himself was not able to accomplish this. But his subordinate, Captain M'Clure, who, in his ship Investigator, had been by an accident separated from him, after awaiting in vain for some time the appearance of his chief, took the command and the whole business into his own hands. Continually in the history of American discovery, as in the history of wars, does it occur that disobedient but daring commanders meet with the chief successes.

M'Clure in the course of a summer pushed along the edges of the north coast of Russian America. I may here remark, as an almost universal fact in the north, that the easiest passages were everywhere close along the edges of the land, and not in the open expanse of the seas. The mainland is sooner warmed through by the summer sun than the mass of deep water, and the ice is first melted there. The streams of the interior, whose temperature is somewhat higher also, in pouring down to the shore melt the ice around. Finally, the icebergs which dip deep into the water cannot come so near the shallow beach, and so they fix themselves firmly to the bottom at some distance from it. In Baffin's Bay, in the Russo-American waters, and in all the other wide straits and gulfs, the centre is usually more filled with huge closely packed masses of ice than the sides, and the ships have to creep along the edges of the mainland.

M'Clure, then, as I said, had in the course of the summer of 1850 penetrated eastwards through the central pack-ice of the Polar Sea, from station to station, and had at last reached the neighbourhood of those parts to which Parry had made his way from the west in 1819, namely, Banks's Land. He approached near to localities often ploughed by English ships, and hoped to penetrate to them, and so accomplish the circumnavigation of America. But amidst these hopes he was frozen in upon the south side of the same strait on whose northern bank, thirty years before, the equally strong hopes entertained by Parry had been wrecked in the ice. It was only by help of sledges over the frozen strait that he was able to reach again from the west "Winter Harbour," the same bay in which Parry, in 1820, coming from the east, had wintered; and again he left letters there in order to apprise any European arriving at the place of his presence and his head-quarters. This was in October, 1850. And this period must be regarded as the actual date of the discovery and completion of the passage around America.

While M'Clure waited in vain two summers and winters in his blocked-up vessels for the watery gates to open, a couple of ships had, in fact, arrived from the other and westerly side through Baffin's Bay and Barrow's Straits, at Parry's former winter quarters. These were the ships Resolute and Intrepid, commanded by Captain Kellett, who belonged to Sir Edward Belcher's expedition. Kellett could no more proceed further westward with his ships than M'Clure eastward. He soon, however, learned the vicinity of the latter from the letters found, which, after the custom of Arctic navigators, he had, as before mentioned, strewed on the neighbouring shores and hidden under signal posts in the ice. In the spring of 1853, Kellett sent a sledging party westward, over the ice of Banks's Strait, to seek for M'Clure. It was the afternoon of April 6, a memorable day in the annals of American discovery. All on board the Investigator, M'Clure's ship, was still. His men haggard, wasted, weakened by hunger, sickness, cold, and hardships of all kinds, had just been preparing a grave for one who had died. They perceived in the east on the ice a dark moving point. They conjectured it at first to be a bear or some other of the wild beasts who were their wonted companions and visitors. The dark spot came nearer. It was a man! and behind him came other human forms and the barking of dogs. These strangers, whom they gazed on in amaze, were Englishmen. They announced themselves as Lieutenant Pim and comrades, the leaders of the sledge party despatched by Kellett.

An indescribable scene followed when the news flew like lightning amongst the cabins and sick berths of the vessel. Many at first declared it a joke, an error, or a vision. Their minds seemed bewildered and incapable of taking in the truth of what they heard. At least when the reality, in the shape of the said Lieutenant Pim sprang on board the ship, all feelings found vent in a loud cheer of delight, and " from all corners and crannies of the ship pressed forth the sick, the speechless, the lame, and the blind, as speedily as their weak and frostbitten limbs would bear them' (I use here the words of an eye-witness), " to see the messenger of Heaven, to put their ear to the mouth that addressed them, and to shake his hand."

The north-west passage was thus decisively discovered. For the FIRST TIME European sailors, coming from opposite quarters of the world, could shake hands on the uppermost ice-capped crown of the far-stretching statue of America. The whole Continent had been sailed round, all save a very small intervening portion, and even on this small portion, as they traversed it by a bridge of ice, they had at least salt water under their feet. Now, first, it could be said that the work begun by Columbus nearly four hundred years before had been completed; and, in pointing to that meeting of the Arctic voyagers, I here conclude the historical picture of the great work which I have endeavoured in a narrow compass to sketch.

CHAPTER VI.

CONCLUDING OBSERVATIONS ON THE RESULTS OF THE DISCOVERY OF AMERICA TO COMMERCE, NAVIGATION, SCIENCE, RELIGION, AND POLITICS.

Introduction of European Diseases—Changes in the Condition and Habits of the Natives of America—Destruction of the American Civilisation—Extinction of the Red Race—Development of new Races—Changes in the Aspect of Nature, and in the Climate through the Cultivation of the Soil and the Introduction of new Animals and Plants: Sugar, Coffee, Cotton, Negro Slavery— Spread of American Plants and Animals in Europe: Potatoes, Tobacco, Maize, Medicines, Turkeys—Changes of Political and Commercial Power and Hegemony in Europe—Zenith of the Power of the Portuguese and Spaniards, and its Decline—Decline of Italian Commerce; of German Commerce; of the Hanse Towns—Freedom of the Netherlands—Rise of the English—Influence on Sciences—Cosmology—Astronomy—Botanical Gardens—Menageries—Natural Sciences—Ethnography—History of Man—Impulse to Invention—Increased moral and physical Mobility of European Nations—Modern Languages and Literature—Spread and Stability of the Christian Religion.

NEITHER the renowned march of Alexander the Great to Asia, nor the noisy deeds of the Crusaders, nor even the destructive eruptions of Alaric or Ghengis Khan, have been so important, nor have had such consequences for humanity, as the quiet voyage of Columbus with his three small vessels across the ocean.

Three hundred and seventy years have elapsed since that event took place, and its consequences, the impulse which it gave to mankind, the good and the evil to which it has led, have had time to become developed. They are of so vast and powerful a nature, that he who shall attempt to speak of the incidents and results of that Herculean work of the maritime nations in the narrow compass of a chapter, appears to be standing before a Chimborazo which he wants to climb in an hour, before an ocean of occurrences which he wants to empty with a nutshell, or to sound with an inch rule.

Before Columbus and Vasco da Gama — to speak within bounds — not more than the sixth part of the land and water superficies of our globe was known to the civilised nations. They dwelt on this sixth part, as it were, upon a large island. They were islanders who knew nothing of the rest of the world. For thousands of years they had moved about and played their parts on this narrow stage. The much-dreaded ocean which surrounded the so-called *Orbis terrarum*, its powerful tides and waves, and the storms which raged upon it, shut men up in their island as with a wall or barrier of clouds, and our unskilled, prejudiced, and timid forefathers sat within this barrier like prisoners in a cage.

It was Columbus who opened the door of this cage, who pierced the wall, and threw down the barrier of prejudices. He smoothed the wild ocean, and transformed it from an impediment into the grand arena of commerce for which the Creator had intended it. The island called world was, so to say, frozen in before Columbus. He thawed the ocean, poured oil upon it, and set all around in motion; to such effect, that the most distant things, which till then had seemed unattainable, now were seen to be connected by the most intimate and natural ties.

Let us imagine that for cycles upon cycles a community of thinking beings had dwelt upon one of those spheres of the universe which we call stars, but that suddenly another sphere, a planet or comet, should shoot through space, dip into the atmosphere and the waters of the first star, and, becoming united with it, would thenceforth form a double star. Let us then think of the revolution such an occurrence would produce in the condition of the old star, and we can then picture to ourselves the state of things on our earth before and after Columbus.

America rose out of darkness like as if it had been a new planet joined on to the old. From the first, this was felt to be the case. "He gave us a new world," were the pithy words which King Ferdinand himself wrote down for Columbus's tomb. In this inscription all is comprised. It is now my task to develop in as few words as possible the full meaning of this laconic epitaph.

In this attempt I could, and indeed I ought to, go through the entire history of the last four hundred years, and show, step by step, how the importance of the ocean and of America has grown in ever-increasing proportions up to the present day; how, since the time of Columbus, scarcely anything has taken place with us without the ocean and America glimmering in the background; and how at present there can be scarcely any change in the moral condition of any part of the globe which is not interwoven, so to speak, with American or oceanic elements.

But, as I have said, I must be brief, and endeavour at once to seize the points of all those facts and events which are most characteristic and important.

In this attempt I shall mainly adhere to the following points of view: 1. The effects of the discovery of America on that continent itself; 2. On the trade, general intercourse, and politics of the old world; 3. On the intellectual and moral character of subsequent generations; 4. On science and Christianity.

As America itself was plainly the first to be affected by its discovery, as it experienced the consequences of the meeting of the two worlds earlier, more rapidly, and in a far greater degree than the old "island," I shall begin with that country.

The old population of America, so poor in means of defence, soon succumbed to the stronger and higher-gifted Europeans. Its peculiar civilisation sickened and died in the embrace of a foreign culture, and the seeds of new people and new states were spread over its wide regions. From all sides new inhabitants, new animals, and new plants were introduced. As with the children of the soil, so likewise were the indigenous plants and races of animals in part exterminated, and nature, the whole physiognomy of the land—even the climate—became greatly changed.

The history of the SUBJUGATION and DESTRUCTION of the RED RACE by the WHITE, forms one of the most horrible chapters in the annals of mankind.

Nowhere has less value been attached to human life; nowhere have nations, possessed of superior power, inflicted so pitilessly on their weaker fellow-creatures such fearful acts of cruelty and oppression as in AMERICA.

Nowhere, too, has a race been seen weaker and less capable of offering resistance to its oppressors than the aborigines of that country, whose pulse, according to the experiences of medical men, has twelve fewer beats in the minute than the average pulsation of the inhabitants of the old world. The natives of America have been mowed down like grass, have melted like snow in the hard grasp of the iron knights of Spain.

Possibly the circumstance that the latter found themselves so greatly in the minority amidst the redundant population of the new world may have contributed to make their conduct so terribly severe, their wars so fearfully bloody. In small bodies, they were often only enabled to save themselves by the most unflinching courage. They had everywhere to gain their ends by the employment of desperate means, and in their situations of difficulty they gave way to the passion of merciless destruction.

They accustomed themselves to exterminate the Indians like birds of the forests, and they took to their aid savage animals, the fearful bloodhounds, some of which were so distinguished for their capacity to worry that the kings of Spain granted them pay and rations like their warriors, and whose names, "Berecillo" and others, have been handed down to posterity in the annals of Spain like the names of their masters, the Pizarros and consorts.

As food for cannon in the sanguinary battles, with the steel and under the axes of their unlawful executioners, by the teeth of their savage war-hounds, and, if all these did not do the work quick enough, in the flames of huge pyres, hundreds of thousands of the original inhabitants of America came to a dreadful end. Still more met their death in cruel bondage, as slaves, driven to the performance of work more arduous than any to which they had ever been accustomed.

They were yoked to the plough, forced to penetrate into the bowels of the earth to search for gold, to dive to the bottom of the sea to bring up pearls; they were abused as beasts of burden, made to carry the Spanish officers, their baggage, their cannon, over endless mountains, across bogs, and through forests of vast extent.

Thus hosts upon hosts met their death, and those who escaped the horrors of war, and, as slaves, did not sink under the lashes of their taskmasters, were carried off by disease.

Many of the European diseases, particularly the smallpox, attacked the Indians with a deadly force. It seemed as if these OLD European pests in their contact with the NEW race were, like the Europeans themselves, possessed of a peculiarly destructive power. They raged amongst the people of the new world like fire amongst the dry herbage of the prairies.

The sufferings and the torments which burst upon

the poor Americans from the Pandora's box which the Spaniards opened upon them, were so unsupportable to this people, that even hope flew away from the bottom of that box, and unable to bear the sight of these terrible men, their steel and fire, suicide became general. It was seen to spread in America like an epidemic, to an extent far beyond all parallel in the history of any other people. The entire populations of islands driven to despair, sought in death a release from their sufferings, and whole families, bidding farewell to their beautiful island homes, cast themselves from the rocks into the sea.

And this did not occur in the time of the Spaniards only. The Portuguese, the English, and the French, who followed the Spaniards to other regions of America, did not display a much gentler spirit; and as their advent was accompanied by many of the same evils and terrors, the spectacle of whole populations committing suicide has, down to modern times, been repeated in other parts of the country.

On the Mississippi and the Missouri, when the Europeans reached the sources of these rivers, and surrounded the tents of the native hunters; when their diseases spread amongst them, and wolves and foxes penetrating into their tents devoured the dying; in those regions, too, the remnants of nations filled with despair sought relief in self-destruction. Entire tribes vanished thus in anguish and in terror of Europeans.

However violently the old conflicts of the American tribes may have raged amongst themselves (according to what we are told), yet they can have been but as child's play in comparison with the scourge of war which the Europeans let loose upon them. For, despite these ancient animosities, we found America occupied in every valley and in every corner by a cheerful people. But when the Europeans had completed their work of discovery and colonisation, in many broad regions the aborigines had been trodden down and had vanished like autumn flowers when winter comes.

A few decenniums after the first voyage of Columbus, the statements of the former great numbers of the Indians seemed incredible and fabulous. The Jesuit Charlevoix reports that only one hundred years from the commencement of the French conquest no more than the twentieth part of the original inhabitants remained. On this side the Mississippi, in lands half as large as Europe, no further TRACE of them is found.

Those American people in whom a peculiar civilisation had begun to be developed were interrupted in their growth and stifled in their childhood. The annihilating blows of the Spanish *conquistadores* fell more especially on the supporters of that civilisation than on the masses of the people. The heathen augurs, the old regal races, the distinguished men of the country, and the teachers of the people, were hunted down in Mexico and Peru more than the common man. And their works of art were destroyed, and their hieroglyphic writings burnt by Christian priests.

The masses who remained were robbed, so to speak, of their brains and their eyes, of those organs by means of which a kind of higher education had been, and could alone continue to be, imparted to them. The Europeans, who neither adopted their language nor customs, had no power to give them anything in place of what they had lost.

The natives forgot their ANCIENT knowledge and arts, without acquiring NEW. They scarcely acquired a habit, feeling, or instinct of civilisation. Their old heathen worship was exchanged for a grotesque Catholicism and the coarsest Christianity. At the present day they speak their old language, as in the time of Cortez, and even now they seem to us to be the creatures of another world.

In many districts of America, in consequence of the irruption of Europeans, the natives became more completely savages that they had been before; this was the case, for instance, with the tribes spread over the wide prairies of the Mississippi, the endless pampas of Patagonia, and the La Plata territory. In former times, the latter lived as peaceful pedestrians in the society of dogs and herds of guanacos that they had tamed.

But when the Europeans came and brought over the horse, the races of hoofed animals increased like the sands on the shore; and when, in consequence, these tribes learned to ride, their habits and customs became entirely changed. They became equestrian robbers, far more active and much wilder than they had been before.

The horned cattle, too, which had been introduced into the country, became wild and spread over vast districts. It was the same with dogs, which, in many places, were transformed into thoroughly savage animals, associating with wolves and jaguars. Similar changes took place in pigs, which, in the course of time, became transformed into entirely peculiar races of wild swine, their nature and the shape of their bodies altering to such a degree that nothing like them had ever before been seen in America, nor yet in Europe.

European animals increased to such an extent in some of the regions of America, that they even altered the aspect of the country, revolutionising the character of the soil and plants. From the plains, for example, over which wild horses in thousands scampered, many peculiar

American plants and bushes disappeared. But other grasses which resisted their tread took their place, and became masters of the soil. Thus many large strips of bushland were transformed into useful pastures.

The class of insects, too, was just as much affected as the vegetation. Even the habits of indigenous birds and beasts of prey, like those of the Indians, became changed. And in many districts, hawks, kites, jaguars, and pumas, increased in proportion to the increase of carrion.

But the European conquerors and settlers, and the iron to which their hands were accustomed, did far more than their animals to alter the nature of the new world. Their ploughs, their axes, and their deadly firelocks brought about in certain districts a state of things entirely new.

The American forests, which had hitherto known only the weak stone hatchet of the Indians, were soon thinned by iron axes and the sharp teeth of saws; and whole ranges of mountains in Mexico and elsewhere were in a short time robbed of their beautiful primeval woods. Here and there, the climate in consequence became greatly modified, and moist districts changed into dry. In many places a noisome aridity obtained.

The plough and the spade, which followed the destructive axe, revolutionised still further. They transformed the natural wilderness into an artificial garden, and in Canada and the Brazils the climate was gradually improved and made milder, although the first turning up of the soil produced peculiar diseases and fevers.

Some of the plants which had been long cultivated in the old world and brought over to the new—for instance, the vine from Europe, the tea and spice-plants from Asia, for which it was hoped to gain new ground in tropical America, have resisted all efforts to make them thrive. Despite the similarity of latitude and climatical conditions, the nature of the new world appears to be opposed to these and some other forms of vegetation, and for some reasons, still unexplained, she refuses them the right of citizenship.

Many other cultivated and nutritious plants and fruit-trees of the old world the new has willingly adopted, and even improved in quality. Our wheat succeeds admirably in Southern, as well as Northern America. Several kinds of fruit, too, as oranges, apples, and peaches, flourish in many districts and climates of America; whilst lemons, pears, and apricots thrive not so well. Peach-trees are found in all parts of the new world; in Chili, in Buenos Ayres, and the United States they grow everywhere luxuriantly, and the fruit is finer than in its old Persian home.

Africa and the South Sea islands have likewise sent useful presents to the great continent lying between them: Asia sent the banana, and Otaheite the bread-tree.

Much more important, however, has it turned out for America, and indeed for the world's commerce, that she has so readily adopted those remarkable plants in regard to civilisation and trade, the sugar-cane, the coffee-tree, and cotton-plant, to which rice may be added, and that soon after the discovery of the country such extensive regions were set apart for their cultivation.

Although derived from Asia and Africa, they have taken root in America to such an extent that we are now almost accustomed to look upon them as American products. Sugar has become in such a preponderating manner the staple article of the West Indies, that they have been named *par excellence* the "sugar islands." Coffee is become the life-blood of Brazilian trade, and the importance of cotton is brought more prominently forward than ever in consequence of the civil war now raging in America.

For America itself these plants are especially remarkable, because with them the sable inhabitants of Africa have wandered into the country, and taken the place of the diminishing natives. After Columbus, Africa, like Europe, crossed the Atlantic Ocean, but, to be sure, poor Africa did not willingly go to sea. By her hard-hearted sister and neighbour, Europe, ill-treated and enslaved, she was dragged over to the new world in chains and fearful sufferings. Before the discovery of America, European slave-hunts in Africa and the trade in negroes had already begun. But without America, on whose soil negroes thrived just as well as coffee and sugar, this iniquitous trade would never have obtained that enormous importance and extension which we have seen.

Together with the sanguinary and pitiless extirpation of the natives of America, the dragging of Africans to that country must be reckoned as the most terrible, most iniquitous, and ever to be lamented consequences of Columbus's discovery. Each of these abominable misdeeds and crimes, committed for centuries by the maritime nations of Europe, has produced results equally fearful as regards the lot of the victims, and, be it said, the morals of the cruel evil-doers. A celebrated author has observed, that for the wealth and the gifts of the new world mankind has paid a high price in general morality, and that the benefits have been purchased by the misery, the tears, and the blood of one hundred thousand human beings sacrificed yearly. In making this reflection, the author's eyes were fixed on those two just-named black and fearful pages in the history of the nations who discovered America.

These cursory remarks on the events under consideration, in their bearings on the ONE side of the ocean, must here suffice. In passing over to the OTHER side, to Europe, it seems to me best that I should again begin with the interchange of plants and animals, and the influences on our habits and customs resulting therefrom; that I should then proceed to consider the political and commercial changes, and lastly conclude with pointing out the altered position of Christianity, of civilization, of sciences, and the highest interests of humanity.

When Europe, originally poor in natural products, had received, through Demetrius and Triptolemus, wheat; through Bacchus, the vine; cherries through Lucullus; and the silkworm through the Emperor Justinian; and when, on other occasions, she had received a few more plants and gifts valuable as food or luxuries from teeming Asia, she obtained nothing new of like value until the discovery of America.

Until the time of Columbus Europe was greatly in Asia's debt; but since that time she owes so much to America that it becomes a question whether, in the last three hundred years, she has not been more indebted to the new world than to the seat of paradise, since the creation of this earth. In this Asiatic paradise there was neither potatoes, nor Indian corn, nor tobacco, nor many other of those American plants which have gained so great a spread, and have produced such extraordinary and lasting results amongst us.

The introduction of the potato alone has made the discovery of America of more importance to posterity than all the rich gold and silver mines of Peru, although, as we shall soon see, the latter have been the cause of many remarkable political revolutions. The potato is a vegetable quite peculiar to America, indigenous there as well in the north as in the south. It is one of the wholesomest and most admirable articles of food, and it is not the least of its good properties that it is day after day agreeable to every palate.

It succeeds well and can be propagated readily in every kind of soil, and almost in every quarter of the globe. It can be cultivated at small expense, suits the fields well, and, until the latest times at least, has not been subject to disease.

In consequence of these and other invaluable properties, when once those prejudices, which even the most beneficial innovations have always to encounter, were overcome, the potato spread both in and out of Europe in a manner without parallel in the history of any other nutritious vegetable.

It has travelled from America, through Europe, through Asia and Siberia, to Kamtschatka, thus making the circuit of the globe, causing everywhere in its progress noiseless revolutions, but not the less remarkable and, in general, beneficial.

Since the time when the Englishmen Hawkins and Raleigh brought over these American roots, periods of scarcity and famine have been much less destructive, and the population of many countries consequently has greatly increased. The potato, too, has brought cultivation and inhabitants into many poor mountainous districts of Europe.

In Germany, the culture history of many of the sandy regions in the north begins with the introduction of this vegetable, which, for example, has had more to do with the history of the Mark Brandenburg and the growth of Prussia than at first sight appears.

Another of America's gifts, not less valuable in many parts of the old world, is that celebrated corn called maize—a name derived from the language of the Antilles—which Columbus brought to Spain in returning from his third voyage, and which, in his life-time, was eagerly cultivated in that country.

From the oldest times this plant has formed a national and staple article of food in America. Its culture has been observed amongst all the aborigines of that country, as well in the north as in the south. This nutritious plant was eagerly received by many of the European nations, and at present, in many parts of Italy, Turkey, and

Southern Germany, it is the principal corn to be seen in the fields, and has become a favourite, indeed national, article of food.

With the introduction of another American plant, a most peculiar Indian custom has spread, and indeed become firmly rooted amongst us. On his first voyage, Columbus observed with astonishment the natives of his island, San Salvador, sitting idle on the beach, inhaling and puffing out again the smoke of a burning weed. The reeds by means of which they brought the hot smoke into their mouths they called "*tabaco,*" and from this has been derived the name of that remarkable plant, which, like the American potato, has wandered from land to land, making the journey round the world.

The Spanish and Portuguese sailors were the first to adopt the Indian custom of intoxicating themselves with the leaves of this narcotic plant. But the English cultivated it in their colonies sooner than any other European people, and they have done the most to promote its spread. They and the French introduced this plant into European gardens, where it was cultivated by botanists and apothecaries, who looked upon it as a wonderful curative remedy, called it a royal plant, and pronounced it to be a panacea in a hundred forms of disease. In France and England smoking first came into fashion at the courts, and tobacco received the name of the

"Queens' weed," after the Queens Elizabeth of England and Catherine de Medici of France.

At a later date smoking was introduced by English soldiers and travellers into Russia; and at the commencement of the seventeenth century English and Dutch navigators had carried the custom to all parts of Asia and Africa.

Although smoking was subsequently forbidden by many European rulers, and in spite of the severe punishments, even mutilations and death, which many Asiatic czars and pashas inflicted on those who indulged in tobacco, nevertheless the invention of the American red skins spread in all directions in an astounding manner until it made the circuit of the globe. It was welcomed by all the races of men, with red or black, white or yellow skins, by all nations and ranks, barbarous or civilised, by high and low, anthropopagi or eaters of vegetables; and in the tents of the Arabs and Tartars, as well as in the palaces of sultans and great moguls, the custom soon prevailed.

The variety of tastes in the human race has become proverbial. There is no exception to this rule so universal and remarkable as that in favour of this American weed and Indian custom. In the taste for tobacco and in passionate indulgence in its use all mankind are in harmony.

If we consider what a powerful influence tobacco has had upon the health and habits of men, on agriculture, on our state governments, and on politics, we may in truth say that through this plant alone the discovery of America has produced results of a most astonishing character in all the other quarters of the globe.

Smoking has caused our habits to become in many ways less sociable, and has greatly injured family life. By men withdrawing to envelop themselves in smoke, the intercourse of the sexes became loosened. And as tobacco diminishes the appetite but increases thirst, taverns and coffee-houses, and other establishments for the sale of beer and wines, came into fashion. We have to thank the discovery of America for much of that kind of so-called sociability to be found in places of public resort. Had there been a Roman plebs after the time of Columbus, "*Tabac et circenses*," and not "*Panem et circenses*," would have been the cry.

America, the home of tobacco, has further continued to be its greatest producer. But it has been cultivated too in other countries—in Asia, Europe, and Africa—and the agriculture of many extensive districts has consequently been greatly changed. Many branches of industry and trade which were unknown before the introduction of tobacco have since become prevalent amongst us.

Since that time, too, many countries and provinces, our knowledge of which was very slight, have become of importance through the cultivation of that plant. It has caused many towns and ports to flourish, and as the rulers of states soon saw in the astonishing demand for tobacco a means of increasing their revenues by taxing it as a luxury or by monopoly of its sale, it has played an important part in the laws and fiscal arrangements of almost every country.

Potatoes, maize, and tobacco are the most prized gifts which we have received from the American flora. But we have only to think of the pine-apple, now in all our hot-houses, and of such generally admired flowers and plants as azaleas, dahlias, mongolias, sun and passion flowers, asters, fuchsias, and the amaryllis, which adorn our gardens, to become aware how much we owe to the exertions of Columbus, Cortez, and their followers, in bringing over to Europe the seeds, bulbs, and cuttings of these and many other plants now become naturalised amongst us.

Many of the luxurious products of America cannot be made to thrive with us. But commerce brings them to Europe in such vast quantities, that there are few warehouses and store-rooms without them. I will here only mention the nourishing and aromatic fruit from which a favourite beverage is prepared, which Cortez was the first European to taste when received by Montezuma as his guest in Mexico. It was subsequently introduced by the Spaniards into Spain, and the old Aztec name "*chocolatl,*" has been received with but little change into every language.

The chocolate-tree or cacao, the delicious vanille creeper, and some other spice and aromatic plants, are exclusively American products, so thoroughly belonging to that country that it has been found impossible to bring them to perfection in any other part of the globe. With several plants belonging to the American tropics this has, however, not been the case. In Africa (in addition to maize), the cassada plant, the pine-apple, capsicum, and the precious nopal, or Indian fig-thistle, on which the cochineal insect breeds, thrive admirably; and these American gifts have long been cultivated by the negroes, and some of them are now likewise cultivated by the French in Algiers.

Although soon after the discovery of America many Europeans died of peculiar diseases brought over from that country (amongst the rest even a monarch, Francis, king of France), the American woods have on the other hand filled our apothecaries' shops with valuable medicines.

I shall here only call attention to a few, known amongst us by their ancient American names: for instance, the copaiva balsam, sassaparilla, sassafras (found everywhere in that country, and which once was in such favour with our sick that whole shiploads were brought over to Europe); further, the precious wood from Guayana, quassia, jalap, ipecacuanha, and lastly, the wonderful quinine, one of the most powerful restorative remedies which Heaven has granted for human debility, and which is found only in the forests of Peru.

The old inhabitants of America were great botanists, and well acquainted with the curative properties of their plants, and we have learned a great deal from them. But it would be necessary to make extensive studies, and to deliver a course of lectures on the subject, if we would collect and communicate all that European physicians, apothecaries, and the sick owe to America, and point out how the ancient American knowledge has, since the time of Columbus, been instilled into our minds and mixed up with our concerns.

America stretches out between two wide oceans, and, just within the tropics it is broken up into numerous islands and narrow isthmuses. Thus, in contrast to the broad mass of Africa in like latitudes, it has a humid climate, a superabundance of rivers and rainy districts. It consequently teems with vegetable wealth; but in variety of races of animals it is far behind the old continent.

Whilst from America's thick and inexhaustible primeval forests new wonders of vegetation have continually come to us down to the present day (I have only to point here to the queen of flowers, the splendid Victoria Regia), our homesteads, on the contrary, have received from thence but one domestic animal, the so-called turkey. In many parts of Europe, particularly in the Danubian Provinces, where it gets its favourite food, Indian corn, this fowl thrives and increases to a great extent; yet for size and beauty of plumage, and, I may add, for the delicacy of flesh, our European specimens are not to be compared to those in the woods of America.

After these remarks on maize, tobacco, potatoes, ipecacuanha and turkeys, as well as on the changes they have caused in our fields, our kitchens, our *materia medica*, and in our habits and customs, I must beg the reader to mount with me into a higher region, to take a survey of the great political and commercial revolutions the discovery of America has produced.

In the beginning it appeared as if all the gain by this event was to fall to the share of Spain and Portugal. The rulers of these two countries, between whom the Pope had divided the globe like an apple, soon began to boast that in their realms the sun never set. Portugal attained to such an extent of power and glory as has seldom been equalled by any other nation of like numerical amount, and never so suddenly acquired. For a considerable time the Portuguese were the boldest and most skilful sailors of Europe, and the heroic deeds they performed inspired the imaginations of poets.

And Spain, which in the ten years succeeding the discovery of America had increased the number of its ships from a few hundreds to more than a thousand, and into which country all the treasures of Mexico and Peru were poured, soon became, under its monarchs Charles V. and Philip II., the terror of our quarter of the globe. For some time Spain was the most powerful state in Europe. Her soldiers, accustomed to all climates, and to brave dangers and difficulties of every kind, were in the sixteenth century the most valiant and most dreaded warriors. Wherever the Spanish regiments appeared, says Jetter, "upright like tapers, with stern looks, and, how great soever their numbers, marching as with one vast tread, there the ground trembled, on this, as well as on the other side of the Atlantic Ocean, and people's hearts shrivelled up within them." It seemed to them " as if the sky was hidden behind a black cloth, which hung down low above their heads."

It appeared, indeed, as if Spain was to have command not only of America, not only of Europe, but of the whole world. She reached the summit of her power in the year 1580, when Philip II. took also possession of Portugal, with all its dependencies in the Brazils, in the East Indies, and other parts of Asia.

But scarcely had Spain reached this summit of power than she began to decline. The seeds of decay had long been within. She had shot up too rapidly, and even during her growth was like a hollow tree.

The poisonous seeds, the destroying evil rooted in part in the constitution which meanwhile Spain had received on its own account, as well as on account of its colonies in America.

Before the victories over the Moors, and the discovery of America, Spain had been a complex of vigorous states possessing very liberal constitutions. It contained a number of industrious towns, which were almost independent in regard to their municipal affairs, like our free German Imperial cities, and in which hand-works and manufactures flourished. The state of things at that time in Spain may be compared to the Confederation of the United Netherlands, or of Switzerland.

But with the conquest of Granada, and the union of all these states and towns into one empire and under one head, all those separate constitutions were gradually thrown overboard. Centralisation levelled in Spain, as it has everywhere done.

When the nation as conquerors went beyond its borders; when the bravest of its sons fought in Italy, in Africa, in Germany, and Flanders, and lastly in America, the military spirit gave birth to a decided despotism in the monarchs, and these, whilst the best blood of the people was being spilt abroad, undermined at home, and at length destroyed the old foundations of the constitution.

With the discovery of America and its gold and silver mines, a thirst for gold spread amongst the population. The Spaniards consequently neglected the preservation of their civil freedom, and with it, too, the cultivation of those surest sources of wealth and happiness, productive labour in agriculture, mechanical arts and trade.

The Emperor Charles, in his celebrated war against the towns, destroyed the freedom and the bloom of the Spanish municipal institutions, just at the time when Cortez conquered Mexico. Amidst the noise of arms, and the greed of discovery and conquest, liberty, industry, and mechanical arts received a withering blow.

"Not to him who plunders it does the world belong, but to him who cultivates it with the sweat of his brow." It is not the glittering coins and precious metals which form the basis of their welfare, but industry and knowledge are the true supports of the power and prosperity of nations. The Spaniards came to forget these truths in a remarkable degree, and partly in consequence of their grand conquests in America.

The same glowing zeal for their faith, which had inspired them with the power to expel the Moors, and filled them with enthusiasm in crossing the ocean, in overleaping its bounds, became fanaticism, and gave birth to that monster, the Inquisition. This inquisition, originally intended to act against the descendants of Jews and Moors for the pure-keeping of the Christian faith, by degrees turned against every freedom of thought, every liberty of action, against science and art; and, as it at last was used to confiscate honestly gained wealth and to plunder industry, it became the most fearful aid to despotism, the most appalling instrument with which tyrants have ever oppressed, lamed, and paralysed a people. The narrow-minded system of government which the kings of Spain had established at home, they also introduced throughout their American colonies. The full power of the nation was granted no field for display in the new world. Nothing was allowed to be undertaken except in the name of the government; and in Spain certain privileged places only were permitted to trade with the colonies. In the several provinces of America, no interchange of goods was allowed. The one dared not supply the wants of another; whatever each required had to be brought direct from the mother country.

Many agricultural plants were forbidden to be introduced into America. The great ocean, which seemed to invite freedom of commerce, was put under lock and key, as it were, like an inland canal with its sluices. Only at certain times, and in certain prescribed courses, were the three-masters allowed to sail, and then with a regularity like that of the Dutch Treck-schuyts.

The vast Pacific Ocean the Spanish kings tried to turn into a *mare clausum*—to make of it an inland lake. Every year they sent from Acapulco one or two ships over to Asia. The cargoes which they took, and those which they brought back were always alike, according to fixed orders; and even the directions in which the vessels steered continued for two hundred years always the same. All foreign nations were absolutely forbidden to enter into the new world.

It is plain that regulations such as these amongst European nations, so little resembling the Chinese, could not be maintained for any length of time, that the authors of such a system in reality were preparing their own ruin. When Spain no longer possessed any flourishing towns, produced nothing suited to America's wants, it had to purchase of other industrial peoples those things which itself and colonies required. As it would not allow other Europeans the least share in its trade, it drove them to extremities, induced them to turn pirates, to lay in wait for the silver fleets and plunder them of their wealth. The colonies, too, being allowed no intercourse with one another, and being obliged to purchase in the mother country at fixed and exorbitant prices the goods they required, naturally grasped at any means to procure them from other nations who offered them on far cheaper terms. Thus an extensive system of smuggling was called into life, which nothing sufficed to check.

In a short time, not a twentieth part of the goods which were transported from Spain to America were produced in the former country. Nineteen parts of every twenty came from Italy, Germany, France, and the Netherlands.

According to the calculation of the historian Robertson, the American gold and silver mines produced yearly the value of from six to seven million pounds sterling.

In three hundred years, this would have made the enormous sum of two thousand million pounds. Had this money remained in Spain and been advantageously laid out in that country, almost every man might in time have become a small capitalist. But from what has been stated, it may be readily inferred that all this money did nothing to promote the wealth and prosperity of the people. A portion of it was paid to English smugglers, another portion came into the hands of English, French, and Dutch buccaneers, and the money that actually reached Spain did not remain there. The indolent, arrogant Spaniards, with their pride of birth, saw it slip through their fingers, and circulate amongst the producing and trading nations. It served but to strengthen their rivals and enemies, and their own rebellious subjects, the Netherlanders.

Briefly to recapitulate: through the discovery of America Spain was raised in the first instance to a dazzling and Europe-terrifying height, but ruined in the end, and with it Portugal too.

Just the reverse, however, was the result of that event on neighbouring kingdoms and peoples—on France, England, and the Netherlands. In consequence of the discovery of America, in the first instance, they were thrown into the background; but in the end they emancipated themselves, partly by means of America and the ocean, from Spanish supremacy, and remained the victors.

In the beginning the Kings of Spain pressed hard on France from every side. They destroyed her influence in Germany, drove her from Italy, kept down the Netherlands with their troops, and tried to destroy the freedom of her cities in the same way as they had already done in the cities and provinces of Spain. For some time every nation was consumed by jealousy and dread of the Spanish supremacy, and even England, when her Queen Mary gave her hand to Philip, the ruler of Spain, seemed, like the Netherlands, about to become a dependency of that empire, and to fall under the tyranny of the inquisition.

But the rise of England under Elizabeth, of the Netherlands under William of Orange, and the fall of Spanish influence in France through the exertions of Henry IV., were events which took place almost at the same time; and equally contemporary were the growth of powerful fleets in these three countries, and their conquests and colonisation in America; those of France in Canada, of the English in Virginia, and of the Dutch in New York and Brazil.

We are unable to assert that at that time these other nations were much more enlightened, or had adopted more liberal views and principles of trade and political economy than the Spaniards and Portuguese. On the contrary, the French, like the Spaniards, had made their colonies a government affair; and the Dutch, when they became powerful at sea, were just as exclusive and jealous of foreigners as the Portuguese.

All of them—English, French, and Dutch—granted monopolies and privileges, and established companies not only to exclude foreigners, but likewise to prevent their own unprivileged countrymen from trading.

They were all of them, too—of which we have plenty of evidence—no less greedy of gold than the Spaniards and Portuguese. If, instead of the Spaniards, any one of these nations had been the first to get possession of the gold and silver mines of the new world, the fate of this one would have been the same as that of Spain. Not to their self-denial and liberal principles do they owe their success, but to the peculiarity of their position. This position obliged them to some extent to try to find out some better way of going to work. In regard to Spain, they were all of them, as it were, in the opposition, and this forced them all by degrees to develop their national energies. Besides, the best parts of America were already occupied, so that they had to put up with the poorer northern regions, and these could only be turned to account by a laborious cultivation. England in especial owes to its eager rivalry with Spain that aspiring and enterprising character, that inventive industry and perseverance, now so remarkable in its inhabitants, and which originally they did not at all possess. This rivalry ended in placing the rule over the ocean in their hands, and enabled them everywhere to reap where the Spaniards and Portuguese had sown. And like as the poet said to the Romans, "For *you* has Carthage flourished, for *you* has Alexander conquered," so also might the English be told that for them Columbus discovered, Gama sailed, and Magellan sacrificed his life.

The discovery of America and the freedom of the seas proved in the beginning the most detrimental to the trade and prosperity of Central Europe, particularly to that of Germany and Italy.

Until that discovery, both these people, the Italians and Germans, had been—and from the same cause, trade with the East—the most prosperous of our quarter of the globe, as their flourishing commercial ports and republics attested. The Italians had their Genoa, Venice, Florence, and other wealthy cities; whilst the Germans had their commanding Hansa in the north; and in the south, the great emporiums of commerce and exchange, Nürnberg and Augsburg, in which the Rothschilds of that time, the Welsers and Fuggers, resided.

When Spain and Portugal raised their tridents, Venice began to decline; though other circumstances have likewise to be taken into account as contributing to this result. With the fall of Venice and the decrease of the importance of the Mediterranean, the south German cities lost their vitality, and the days of the German Fuggers came to an end.

When England soon afterwards bestirred herself and took part in American enterprises; when she became possessed of an ocean fleet and freed herself from the tutelage of the Hansa, this remarkable confederacy of German towns fell too, and we are justified in saying, partly in consequence of the discovery of America. German trade ceased, not to rise again to importance till later times, and then, to be sure, in another way, and through the aid of America.

At last the Northern powers were drawn into the American whirlpool. Denmark and Sweden sailed across the ocean, and obtained colonies in the new world. And even Russia, from the time of Peter the Great, emerged from its forests, built a fleet, removed its capital from the interior of the country to the sea-coast, and when it had completed its march through Siberia, by this road it too acquired its portion of the new world.

Thus, with the sole exception of Turkey, all the states of Europe were busy on the waters of our planet, and stretching out their arms all round the globe. From this time every European revolution became a world-revolution; every European war, a war all over the earth.

When America at length began to free herself from the rule of Europeans, other principles came back from thence: principles which not only disturbed the power of states, but changed their constitutions and interior organisations.

Beginning with Columbus, when he planted his little

towns in Hispañola, it had been seen that a certain equality of rank is necessary to the founding of a colony. This principle, as old as the American colonies, was loudly pronounced when the free states threw off the English yoke. In their celebrated Declaration of Independence, they proclaimed that "all men are free and born equal." This American phrase and declaration acted like oil upon the flames of the French revolution, and since then, partly receiving it from America, a democratic tendency is perceptible in the human race.

Since the discovery of America, a revolution in the department of science has been no less remarkable than in commerce and politics. Natural history, geography, astronomy, and, in fact, all physical sciences, were the first to derive benefit from that event. Until the age of discovery, natural sciences and geography were confined to very narrow limits. Until then they were cramped by the doctrines of Aristotle, of Pliny, and Ptolemy, whose rule had endured two thousand years! Natural history had made no progress since the days of Aristotle; and no one had dared to question the astronomical system of Ptolemy.

In the middle ages, instead of astronomy, we had astrology; instead of physics, magic; instead of chemistry, alchemy; natural science resembled, so to speak, a mummy tightly swathed in ancient ligaments, which the learned men had handed down from generation to generation as they had received it from the Egyptians and Greeks.

Columbus awakened this chrysalis from its sleep, and caused it to spread its golden wings. Since then it has taken a lofty flight.

Already in his first voyage Columbus began to speculate on the size and the form of the earth, and the thinkers who succeeded him have continued to reason on this subject until we have come to our present accurate conceptions of our planet.

He also, in his first voyage, took careful note of the direction of the winds and the oceanic currents, and the impulse he gave to observation has led by degrees to our present knowledge of the atmosphere and waters around our globe, to the sciences of meteorology and oceanography.

We have to thank Columbus, too, for the first observations on the deflections of the magnetic needle, which laid the foundation of the important science of the earth's magnetism.

Columbus, Cortez, and Magellan, and all the other Spanish and Portuguese conquerors, were careful observers of nature. In the new world they found much to attract their attention, for, if some things were similar to those in Europe, yet none were exactly alike, and the greater number entirely different. Even their military reports were always mixed up with observations on the plants and animals of the new world, and to the gold and pearls and prisoners of war that they sent to their kings, were added marsupials, armadillos, and llamas, and other specimens of transatlantic animals and plants.

These specimens were admired at court, were drawn by artists, and the earliest maps of the world were plentifully adorned with pictures of newly discovered creatures and shrubs.

The idea of zoological gardens came probably direct from America, in imitation of Montezuma, whose large and old-established menagerie Cortez described in his letters to the Emperor Charles V. Until that time, instead of menageries, so-called bear-gardens only had been known in Europe.

Botanical gardens, too, came into fashion soon after the discovery of America. That of Padua was established in 1533, and soon afterwards those of Bologna, Wittenberg, Leipzig, and Zurich.

Collections of transoceanic curiosities soon followed the zoological and botanical gardens, and from them, in the course of time, our rich museums of natural history have grown.

Even European monarchs began to take an interest

in, and to cultivate, natural sciences. For example, the greatest warrior and politician of his time, the Emperor Charles V., was a great lover of nature. In the monastery of St. Justus he derived great pleasure from conversations with learned men on natural history, and his memory is honoured by gardeners for having introduced to Europe one of the most beautiful of flowers, the fragrant carnation.

Without the discoveries in the ocean, merely by the help of Aristotle and the few products of Europe, the natural sciences would certainly never have become that which they now are—the favourite and most cultivated sciences of our time.

Before Columbus, scientific systems and classifications of nature, a Linnæus, a Cuvier, were impossibilities. There could be no connected system of the universe, no conception of a vast organism, of a plan in creation, as long as only a small part of the picture, a few pieces of the great machinery, were known.

If it is true that God created the universe according to a plan, that in this creation all things are in harmony, that there is a chain without breaks, and in which one link passes into another in close connexion—if all this be true, it was as impossible before the time of Columbus to speak of a science of nature as it would be for any one to solve an arithmetical problem without being acquainted with all the factors. Only since the discovery of America have we been able to take a survey of nature's storehouse. If we cannot understand all we see in it, if we are still unable everywhere to perceive the perfect harmony of things, yet, at least, we know what we have before us.

Above all, in consequence of the discoveries of the Spaniards and Portuguese, a great impulse was given to astronomy. What could this science be as long as the other half of the firmament was unknown? as long as it was doubted whether the earth was round or flat? as long as it was believed that our earthly home—this atom, this drop, in the ethereal ocean—formed the chief object of the universe, and that the stars did but fly around it like the sparks around a blacksmith's forge? Since the times of Columbus and Magellan, the earth has been taken from the old postament on which poetry and ignorance had placed it, and shown to float with us like a balloon in illimitable space.

Progress in astronomy, again, made it easier for us to find our way upon this earth. In their old dwelling-place, Europe, the nations knew their way everywhere, as they believed, perfectly well. There was no inducement to find out new methods for taking surveys and for the construction of accurate maps. But the new world was a very labyrinth to the discoverers who found themselves quite unable to know where they were without the aid of charts and maps. Besides, the rivalry of the Portuguese and Spaniards, to whom the new world had been apportioned, spurred them to seek the surest means of ascertaining longitudes and latitudes, and of acquiring correct maps of their possessions.

Nearly all the new methods for ascertaining longitudes have, in the first instance, been tried on the American coasts; and all the inventions for the improvement of the compass, the quadrant, watches, chronometers, and other instruments necessary for land-surveying and navigation, have been called forth with reference to America and other new countries. Such great pains were taken, that in the maps made in the earliest times of discovery we find the outline of Africa and the parts of America already known drawn far more correctly than many parts of Europe—for instance, than the Scandinavian north. But not only to engineers, cartographers, and natural historians were new and vast regions opened by the discovery of America, but likewise to ethnographers and philologists. Before the voyage of Columbus, the investigations of the latter were confined to a comparatively narrow field; for they had never even dreamt of many of the varieties and phases of the human race.

In the transoceanic lands the philologists met with

entirely new classes of languages, with peculiar qualities never till then heard of, and quite different from those in the body of any other language.

To our historians, likewise, perfectly new phenomena were disclosed. In regard to culture-historical developments and moral conditions, they found much to study totally dissimilar to the experiences of the old continent. Now, for the first time, it became possible to speak of a universal history—of a history of the human race.

All other sciences, too, if not immediately affected by the discovery of America, were indirectly advanced by this event, and their stand-points were raised and altered. The daring voyage of Columbus across the ocean had burst many bonds, had dissipated many prejudices, and awakened a new and bold freedom of thought. On all sides the view became extended, and the spirit of inquiry greatly strengthened.

New ideas in one department gave rise to new ideas in another. In the same year in which Columbus died, Copernicus discovered his new system of the universe; in the same year in which Cortez conquered Tenochtitlan, Luther burnt the Pope's bull at Wittenberg; at the time when Frobisher attempted to sail round the north of America, Pope Gregory XIII. improved the calendar. The invention of the telescope in 1590, of the thermometer in 1630, of the barometer in 1647, of the air-pump in 1650, and of other important scientific instruments in the following years, if they had no direct reference to America, were nevertheless links in the great chain of inventions, of which the astrolabes and ships-pumps constructed by the Spaniards and Portuguese were the first.

One of our German historians of America has said with truth: "The most important result of the ocean voyages and discoveries is not the addition to our knowledge of geography *per se*, but the opening in all directions of new channels of reciprocal communication in the interest of all mankind." All the great thinkers and philosophers of modern times—Bacon, Grotius, Leibnitz, Newton, Montesquieu, Locke, and Kant—would probably never have appeared without Columbus, and but for him, in every case, they would have been very different from what they were. It may safely be said that before Columbus, men like them, imbued with the free spirit of investigation, were very rare, but that after him they shone forth in greater numbers, like the stars of the southern heavens.

Even with poetry, with the bloom of our literatures, and with the history of our national languages, the age of discovery and its powerful impulses are more intimately connected than is generally acknowledged. Like as the voyages of the Argonautæ, and the expeditions of the Hellenes to Asia Minor inspired Homer; like as the Crusades inspired Tasso, and the discoveries of Gama in the East Indies set the muse of Camoens in activity, and called forth the classical epic of the Portuguese; so, too, has the Spanish muse been greatly occupied with the adventures and wonders of the new world, and these, in addition to the "Argentina" and "Araucania" of Ercilla, have called into life many another epic.

The bloom-period of Spanish literature followed quick upon the bloom-period of the power of the Castilians, and of their wonderful deeds and sufferings in the new world. In England, too, Shakspeare followed soon upon the sea-heroes of Queen Elizabeth. In writing one of his dramas, "The Tempest," Shakspeare seems to have had a discovery of his countrymen, that of the Bermudas Islands, present to his mind. With the Netherlanders, too, the culminating periods of their power at sea and of their literature followed close upon one another.

The Europeans of whatever country who went over to America, were for the most part sailors, soldiers, farmers, merchants, and other workmen who could speak no other than the so-called "vulgar" languages; the "good Latinists" were rare.

In the colonies and states planted by those men

from the beginning, no other than the vernacular languages were used. In this respect, therefore, the discovery and colonisation of America resembled " a stepping out of the boundaries of the Roman Empire," an emancipation from the trammels of Latin and all connected with it.

Since that time, all the European national languages have travelled round the world; and although, before Columbus, men could get on better by the aid of Latin, yet, after him, the modern languages gradually extended their arms to other hemispheres, and necessarily became an object of zealous study.

Nearly all the accounts of travel, all the historical and geographical works relating to the new world, have been written in the vulgar tongues. There are very few works on America in Latin, not even amongst those which were published at the time when the histories and geographies of many European countries were still written in that classic language. Many of the treatises on those departments of science and knowledge to which the age of discovery gave birth—for example, on navigation, oceanography, the principles of commerce and merchandise—were, from the beginning, written in the national tongues, and have never been subjected to Latin swaddling-clothes.

And not only did the imagination, the thoughts, and

the investigations of great minds receive a loftier and freer impulse, in consequence of the development of the ocean navigation, but likewise to all the concerns of man an increased and general activity was given. All the European nations bordering on the ocean spread their wings soon after the discovery of America, or rather it was not till then that their pinions grew, that the sails of their fleets—so long neglected—were seen to enliven the ocean. Before the discovery of America, marine affairs were scarcely thought of in the states of Europe; but from that time they have formed an important branch of government.

Indeed, it may be said that America, the long-continued work of discovery, and the experiences gained thereby, gave growth and vigour to the navies of Europe. The commanders of the fleets sent by Queen Elizabeth to America, were the heroes who were called upon to oppose the Spanish Armada.

The fish-banks of Newfoundland and other American waters have been the school in which French, Dutch, and English sailors have acquired their skill. The Greenland whale fisheries, and the three centuries of voyages to discover a north-west passage, have had their share, too, in perfecting our mariners.

And also in other ways has America been the nursery of European fleets. Cuba supplied the Spanish docks with the best wood for ship-building. The Portuguese fleets were built almost entirely of Brazilian timber; and even England was for a long time supplied with Brazilian ships.

Moreover, out of her own bosom has America herself sent forth one of the most skilful, brave, and active seafaring people, the Yankees, who are now to be found on every sea, flying with the wind all over the world, as if it were their own domain. If I were to attempt to sum up the characteristics of these Yankees in one word, the one that would best suit is "restlessness."

Our activity, our navigation, our commerce, have, as we have seen, continually grown in value and proportions since the discovery of America, and this event soon gave rise to improved means of communication by land as well as by water. When large three-masters swept backwards and forwards across the ocean, bringing to our ports the products of distant continents in vast quantities, the old pack-horses and mules with panniers no longer sufficed for the transport of these goods into the interior. Nations began by degrees to make their roads as smooth as the ocean. Water-courses were improved, the construction of harbours, canals, and high-roads commenced. It is not irrelevant to the subject we are discussing to observe that the great monarch who had the most to do with the discovery of the new world,

Charles V., was the same who ordered the construction of paved roads in Spain, and who was the first to establish a post communication in Germany and elsewhere.

Every revolution in the navigation of the sea brought about a reform in continental roads (although these reforms often lagged greatly in the rear). Nearly all the inventions for the improvement of locomotion have come from maritime nations—from the English, Dutch, and the Yankees.

When the steam-engine had once been put upon the water to supply the place of the wind, it was naturally soon taught to run and draw upon land, to do the work of horses. Without the discovery of America, without the circumnavigation of the globe, without the entire change of the speed introduced by these events into the movements of man, we should probably not now possess macadamized roads, railways, or telegraphs. Indeed, it may be doubted whether we should have had the convenient foot pavement in our cities to expedite the transaction of business.

America and the ocean are like powerful springs, driving and urging on the great mechanism of modern life. America flourishes in all our gardens, our fields, our towns; and the ocean, with its currents and its tides, penetrates into our inland canals. It is not solely to feed the snorting broods of Amphitrite that Neptune wields his sceptre, he strikes as well at the very root of the earth. His *Quos ego,* far resounding over the briny seas, reaches the ears of rulers as plainly as those of the denizens of mountains and other retired nooks of continents, and moves their hearts. But of all that he has done since Columbus and the Spaniards presented him with a new trident, nothing is of such force and meaning as the altered position to which the ocean has elevated Christianity.

If we consider and compare the position of Christianity, its geographical spread before the discovery of America, with its present position in the world, we must be astonished at the narrow space it formerly occupied.

Despite the exertions and baptising wars of Charlemagne, and despite the Christian migrations in the centuries of the Crusades, it can hardly be said that, from the times of the first Councils ("Consilien") in Asia Minor, Christianity had made any important local progress.

Indeed, it had probably lost more in the South than it had gained in the North. Two great portions of the globe had been lost to the Church—the whole of Western Asia, where the Apostles had travelled as far as India, and the whole north of Africa, where at one time hundreds of Christian towns and bishoprics had flourished.

Even in our small Europe, Christianity was confined in narrower boundaries. The two centuries of efforts on the part of the Crusades had produced scarcely any result. If we sum up their doings, they can be looked upon in no other light than as failures. Indeed, they produced the very contrary of what was intended. Instead of vanquishing the Crescent, and driving it back, these Crusaders drew it out of its hiding-places, and brought it further into Europe. The Mahometan Turks conquered the whole south-east of Europe, Greece, and the countries of the Danube, as far as Vienna; and the Islam-worshipping Tartars ruled Russia to the confines of Poland and Germany. On the other side of the Pyrenees, too, the Koran was to be found close to the Bible.

Before Columbus, the condition of Christianity, after fifteen centuries of conflict, was pitiable. It was confined within a narrow compass, hard pressed, and probably the number of its adherents were fewer than in the days of the Emperors Constantine or Justinian.

It is only since the discovery of America and the ocean paths, that the stability of the Christian religion has become a certainty. Only since then have the words of Christ, "Go ye into all the world and preach the gospel to every creature," become a truth and full of meaning. Since that time Christianity is become a world-wide religion, the faith of the globe. From that time Europe began to understand its mission—namely, to civilise all mankind—and it need no longer be feared that this work of civilisation should retrograde like that of the Macedonians and Romans.

It has been said to be the peculiar mark of the civilisation of modern times, "that all the culture-forms of the Orient, those of the Mussulmans, the Hindus, and the Buddhists, when opposed to the Christian European form, lose all their power, becoming partly subordinate, partly weakened." And that it should be thus we have not to thank those high-born knights with the Cross on their armour, but rather the oft-mentioned navigators and their crews. They, too, had the Cross on their pennants. They, too, sailed forth to conquer Jerusalem. All their undertakings, the whole history of discovery, sprang mainly from the conflict of the Cross with the Crescent. I have said above that in pursuing the Moors the Portuguese were led upon the watery paths, and that the Spaniards, just at the time when they planted the Cross on the walls of the Alhambra, received the impulse to the discovery of America.

These discoveries, therefore, in their cause, in their tendency, and in respect to their object, were mainly religious enterprises. The Christian missionary spirit gave them a colouring, and the pious desire of converting and baptising played as great a part as the greed of land and gold.

The Russians likewise, as I have shown, were led to America by their war with Mahometans, from whose yoke they freed themselves, and whom they pursued in Siberia, as the Portuguese had pursued them in Africa.

The importance of the discovery of America in forwarding the spread of Christianity seems from the first to have been understood by the contemporaries of Columbus. They gave form to their feeling in this respect in a symbolic and very characteristic manner; for in the old maps of the new discoveries of Christopher Columbus, they drew the picture of St. Christopher on the coast of America wading through the surf, and carrying the infant Christ on his shoulders.

Christopherus, the mariner-pilgrim, has carried the mustard-seed to all the shores of the world, and since then Christianity and civilisation in their onward progress may be compared to that wonderful East-Indian tree which derives its nourishment and secures its existence through many hundred channels, dropping its branches down to the earth to take root, again to shoot upwards.

In the foregoing sketch of the consequences of that series of events, deeds, enterprises, and exertions of the bold Europeans, in which Columbus led the way, I have only attempted to seize the most prominent and important points, to plant a few sign-posts, as it were, for the guidance of others. Much that I have omitted the imagination of the reader will supply. He who will study and investigate for himself, will understand more and more why a NEW ERA is dated from the year 1492, why our historians consider the ANCIENT history of man to be then concluded. After the discovery of the new countries, from the time when, in consequence of this discovery, all parts of the world, all its inhabitants, may be said to have commenced a common life, into this life a new and stirring spirit, a new soul — and this a CHRISTIAN soul—was breathed. With justice, therefore, historians date from this time the beginning of MODERN HISTORY.

THE END.

www.ingramcontent.com/pod-product-compliance
Lightning Source LLC
Chambersburg PA
CBHW031333230426
43670CB00006B/335